COLUMBIA COLLEGE CHICAGO

T4-AQP-192

Differentiating Reading Instruction
through Children's Literature

ENTERED JAN 2 2 2010

DATE DUE

Demco, Inc. 38-293

COLUMBIA COLLEGE LIBRARY
600 S. MICHIGAN AVENUE
CHICAGO, IL 60605

DIFFERENTIATING READING INSTRUCTION THROUGH CHILDREN'S LITERATURE

Liz Knowles, Ed.D.

Libraries Unlimited

An Imprint of ABC-CLIO, LLC

A B C ☰ C L I O

Santa Barbara, California • Denver, Colorado • Oxford, England

Copyright 2009 by Libraries Unlimited

All rights reserved. No part of this publication may be reproduced, stored in a retrieval system, or transmitted, in any form or by any means, electronic, mechanical, photocopying, recording, or otherwise, except for the inclusion of brief quotations in a review, without prior permission in writing from the publisher.

Library of Congress Cataloging-in-Publication Data

Knowles, Liz.
  Differentiating reading instruction through children's literature / Liz Knowles.
    p. cm.
  Includes index.
  ISBN 978-1-59158-787-3 (pbk : alk. paper) — ISBN 978-1-59158-788-0 (ebook) 1. Reading. 2. Children—Books and reading. 3. Teenagers—Books and reading. 4. Individualized instruction. I. Title.
  LB1573.K626   2009
  372.41'7—dc22   2009011616

13   12   11   10   9   1   2   3   4   5

This book is also available on the World Wide Web as an eBook.
Visit www.abc-clio.com for details.

ABC-CLIO, LLC
130 Cremona Drive, P.O. Box 1911
Santa Barbara, California 93116-1911

This book is printed on acid-free paper ∞
Manufactured in the United States of America

Copyright Acknowledgments

Excerpts from "The Kids & Family Reading Report™" used with permission of Scholastic Inc.

Excerpts from Russ, S., Perez V., Garro, N., Klass, P., Kuo, A.A., Gershun M., Halfon, N., Zuckerman, B. *Reading Across the Nation: A Chartbook*. Boston, MA: Reach Out and Read National Center. Copyright © 2007.

Contents

Introduction

How often have you heard it said that teaching reading is the responsibility of all teachers? One might even say that it is the responsibility of all adults who are in contact with students in an educational setting. We would like all students to have comfort and confidence with the written word at an early age. Volumes have been written about the teaching of reading, the importance of early literacy, illiteracy data and the results, and aliteracy, which is very common today with young people when there are so many other exciting things to do rather than read.

The first chapter of this book discusses the state of reading today—the data, the test results, and the challenges. Next, in Chapter 2, all aspects of teaching reading including models, methods, and best practices are explored. Chapter 3 deals with issues that affect adolescent success in reading and provides summaries of research. It also offers abundant suggestions for providing differentiated and appropriate reading instruction. Chapter 4 discusses the literature on the effect of brain research on learning to read from such experts in the field as Patricia Wolf, David Sousa, Eric Jensen, and Robin Fogarty, among others. Brain research now provides teachers with materials and classroom activities that promote learning. The whole concept of differentiated instruction is reviewed in Chapter 5 and then adapted to the teaching of reading in Chapter 6. Finally, the future of reading is explored in Chapter 7, which includes helpful organizations and Web sites.

This information is pertinent to those working with early literacy through to those who teach young adults of high school age. Teachers, school librarians, curriculum coordinators, reading specialists, reading coaches, teacher trainers, school administrators, university-level classes on teacher education, program developers, and parents will find useful information in these pages.

Following Chapter 7, lesson ideas are included for various titles. The lesson plans are divided into three sections: PK–3, Grades 4–7, and Young Adult. They are organized by book title, and each lesson has author information, a synopsis, generic discussion questions, curricular connections, and suggested ways to differentiate instruction.

The next section features author information, listed alphabetically by author last name, and includes Web site addresses, interesting facts, and contact information. The book concludes with annotated resources, including all the resources used in this book.

CHAPTER 1

Reading Today—What Does the Research Say?

Educating the nation's children is more challenging than ever. The government has become very involved in directing reading instruction in our nation's schools. With the development of the Reading First program in 2001, schools were led to believe that only a small handful of reading instruction programs were research-based and therefore worth using. Many schools signed up for the government funding provided by Reading First and proceeded to use certain reading programs as directed and made major changes in their reading programs in the hope of achieving success for all students. It is important to begin with a look at the research that is currently available.

The following Fast Facts from the Institute of Education Science of the United States Department of Education's National Center for Education Statistics recently reported these numbers:

> In fall 2008, a record 49.8 million students will attend public elementary and secondary schools. Of these, 34.9 million will be in prekindergarten through 8th grade and 14.9 million in grades 9 through 12. An additional 6.2 million students are expected to attend private schools this fall.
>
> Public school systems will employ about 3.3 million teachers this fall, resulting in a pupil/teacher ratio of 15.3, which is lower than in 2000, when the ratio was 16.0. An additional 0.5 million teachers will be working in private schools this fall, where the pupil/teacher ratio is estimated at 13.0.
>
> There are about 14,200 public school districts containing about 97,000 public schools, including about 4,000 charter schools. There were about 35,000 private schools offering kindergarten or higher grades.
>
> Current expenditures for public elementary and secondary schools will be about $519 billion for the 2008-09 school year. The national average current expenditure per student is around $10,418, up from $9,154 in 2005-06.
>
> Source: http://nces.ed.gov/fastfacts/display.asp?id=372

It is not possible to discuss the current state of reading without including the latest test results from the National Assessment of Educational Progress (NAEP). The next section contains the Executive Summary from the Nation's Report Card on Reading 2007 followed by charts comparing the reading test results of the nation's fourth and eight graders from 1992 to 2007.

Reading skills are improving for both fourth- and eighth-graders, particularly among lower- and middle-performing students. Many student groups made gains in both grades; however, these gains were not always accompanied by significant closing of racial/ethnic and gender gaps.

A nationally representative sample of more than 350,000 students at grades 4 and 8 participated in the 2007 reading assessment. Comparing these results to results from previous years shows the progress fourth- and eighth-graders are making both in the nation and in individual states.

Fourth-graders scored higher in 2007 than in all the previous assessment years. The average reading score was up 2 points since 2005 and 4 points compared to the first assessment 15 years ago. Higher percentages of students were performing at or above the *Basic* and *Proficient* achievement levels in 2007 than in previous years.

The average reading score for eighth-graders was up 1 point since 2005 and 3 points since 1992; however, the trend of increasing scores was not consistent over all assessment years. In comparison to both 1992 and 2005, the percentage of students performing at or above the *Basic* level increased, but there was no significant change in the percentage of students at or above the *Proficient* level.

White, Black, and Hispanic students all scored higher in 2007 than in the first assessment 15 years ago at both grades 4 and 8. However, improvements for minority students did not always result in the narrowing of the achievement gaps with White students. Only the White–Black gap at grade 4 was smaller in comparison to the gaps in 2005 and 1992.

Patterns in improvement for male and female students varied by grade. Scores for both male and female students increased since 2005 at grade 4, but not at grade 8. In 2007, female students scored 7 points higher than male students at grade 4 and 10 points higher at grade 8. These gender score gaps were not significantly different from the gaps seen 15 years ago.

Percentages of students at or above each achievement level for reading, Grade 4, All students [TOTAL]: By jurisdiction, 1992, 1994, 1998, 2000, 2002, 2003, 2005 and 2007

All Students	Year	Jurisdiction	Below Basic	Standard Error	At or above Basic	Standard Error	At or above Proficient	Standard Error	At Advanced	Standard Error
	1992 1	National	37.92	(1.061)	62.08	(1.061)	28.56	(1.222)	6.40	(0.619)
	1994 1	National	39.52	(1.028)	60.48	(1.028)	29.64	(1.090)	7.40	(0.707)
	1998 1	National	37.61	(0.938)	62.39	(0.938)	30.85	(0.859)	7.32	(0.471)
	1998	National	40.35	(1.191)	59.65	(1.191)	29.32	(0.946)	7.05	(0.467)
	2000	National	40.54	(1.351)	59.46	(1.351)	29.45	(1.094)	6.93	(0.578)
	2002	National	36.12	(0.468)	63.88	(0.468)	31.46	(0.440)	7.09	(0.195)
	2003	National	36.60	(0.295)	63.40	(0.295)	31.46	(0.329)	7.68	(0.127)
	2005	National	35.80	(0.308)	64.20	(0.308)	31.50	(0.244)	7.50	(0.127)
	2007	National	32.84	(0.294)	67.16	(0.294)	33.09	(0.319)	7.90	(0.179)

[1] Accommodations were not permitted for this assessment.

Note: Observed differences are not necessarily statistically significant. Detail may not sum to totals because of rounding.

Source: U.S. Department of Education, Institute of Education Sciences, National Center for Education Statistics, National Assessment of Educational Progress (NAEP), 1992, 1994, 1998, 2000, 2002, 2003, 2005 and 2007 Reading Assessments.

Average scale scores for reading, Grade 4, All students [TOTAL]: By jurisdiction, 1992, 1994, 1998, 2000, 2002, 2003, 2005 and 2007

All Students	Year	Jurisdiction	Average Scale Score	Standard Error
	1992 [1]	National	216.74	(0.935)
	1994 [1]	National	214.26	(1.017)
	1998 [1]	National	217.32	(0.779)
	1998	National	214.77	(1.139)
	2000	National	213.36	(1.274)
	2002	National	218.58	(0.420)
	2003	National	218.24	(0.275)
	2005	National	218.98	(0.211)
	2007	National	220.99	(0.264)

[1] Accommodations were not permitted for this assessment.

Note: The NAEP Reading scale ranges from 0 to 500. Observed differences are not necessarily statistically significant.

Source: U.S. Department of Education, Institute of Education Sciences, National Center for Education Statistics, National Assessment of Educational Progress (NAEP), 1992, 1994, 1998, 2000, 2002, 2003, 2005 and 2007 Reading Assessments.

Percentages of students at or above each achievement level for reading, Grade 8, All students [TOTAL]: By jurisdiction, 1992, 1994, 1998, 2002, 2003, 2005 and 2007

All Students	Year	Jurisdiction	Below Basic	Standard Error	At or above Basic	Standard Error	At or above Proficient	Standard Error	At Advanced	Standard Error
	1992 [1]	National	30.51	(0.975)	69.49	(0.975)	29.18	(1.119)	2.93	(0.331)
	1994 [1]	National	30.42	(0.885)	69.58	(0.885)	29.55	(0.914)	2.82	(0.269)
	1998 [1]	National	25.93	(0.881)	74.07	(0.881)	33.18	(0.938)	2.66	(0.365)
	1998	National	26.62	(0.799)	73.38	(0.799)	32.26	(1.054)	2.64	(0.271)
	2002	National	24.51	(0.467)	75.49	(0.467)	32.63	(0.514)	2.78	(0.188)
	2003	National	26.17	(0.259)	73.83	(0.259)	32.22	(0.274)	3.16	(0.083)
	2005	National	27.42	(0.195)	72.58	(0.195)	30.76	(0.203)	2.98	(0.096)
	2007	National	25.96	(0.248)	74.04	(0.248)	31.23	(0.227)	2.77	(0.108)

[1] Accommodations were not permitted for this assessment.

Note: Observed differences are not necessarily statistically significant. Detail may not sum to totals because of rounding.

Source: U.S. Department of Education, Institute of Education Sciences, National Center for Education Statistics, National Assessment of Educational Progress (NAEP), 1992, 1994, 1998, 2002, 2003, 2005 and 2007 Reading Assessments.

Average scale scores for reading, Grade 8, All students [TOTAL]: By jurisdiction, 1992, 1994, 1998, 2002, 2003, 2005 and 2007

All Students	Year	Jurisdiction	Average Scale Score	Standard Error
	1992 [1]	National	260.04	(0.919)
	1994 [1]	National	259.64	(0.826)
	1998 [1]	National	263.63	(0.770)
	1998	National	262.94	(0.756)
	2002	National	264.34	(0.418)
	2003	National	263.29	(0.258)
	2005	National	262.17	(0.180)
	2007	National	262.79	(0.189)

[1] Accommodations were not permitted for this assessment.

Note: The NAEP Reading scale ranges from 0 to 500. Observed differences are not necessarily statistically significant.

Source: U.S. Department of Education, Institute of Education Sciences, National Center for Education Statistics, National Assessment of Educational Progress (NAEP), 1992, 1994, 1998, 2002, 2003, 2005 and 2007 Reading Assessments.

Source: NAEP, The Nation's Report Card: Reading. http://nces.ed.gov/nationsreportcard/pubs/main2007/2007496.asp

These charts of results do not give a continuous report because some years are missing. In general, they state that some scores were significant, but they do not tell which ones. There does not seem to be a pattern. On the whole, things are better, but there is much fluctuation. In recent years, there is not a significant trend—in fact, the standard error is getting lower. The gains over the years have been minimal, and each year it seems that the scores are manipulated a bit to include or exclude certain constituencies. Teaching for high-stakes tests has become a much-debated topic.

We know that there is a direct connection between reading and writing, and clearly that connection needs to be strengthened. In the 2007 National Assessment of Educational Progress in writing, only a third of 8th graders and one-fourth of 12th graders in nationally representative samples were deemed proficient in writing.

In the fall of 2007, the National Endowment for the Arts released the results of a reading study: *To Read or Not to Read: A Question of National Consequence*. Manzo, in *Education Week* (November 19, 2007), claims that this report says that essentially the increasing use of electronic media seems to be to blame for a decline in pleasure reading.

These are the key findings from the report:

Americans are reading less—teens and young adults read less often and for shorter amounts of time compared with other age groups and with Americans of previous years.

- Less than one-third of 13-year-olds are daily readers, a 14 percent decline from 20 years earlier. Among 17-year-olds, the percentage of nonreaders doubled over a 20-year period, from 9 percent in 1984 to 19 percent in 2004.[1]

- On average, Americans aged 15 to 24 spend almost two hours a day watching TV and only seven minutes of their daily leisure time reading.[2]

Americans are reading less well—reading scores continue to worsen, especially among teenagers and young males. By contrast, the average reading score of nine-year-olds has improved.

- Reading scores for 12th-grade readers fell significantly from 1992 to 2005, with the sharpest declines among lower-level readers.[3]

- 2005 reading scores for male 12th-graders are 13 points lower than for female 12th-graders, and that gender gap has widened since 1992.[4]

- Reading scores for American adults of almost all education levels have deteriorated, notably among the best-educated groups. From 1992 to 2003, the percentage of adults with graduate school experience who were rated proficient in prose reading dropped by 10 points, a 20 percent rate of decline.[5]

The declines in reading have civic, social, and economic implications—Advanced readers accrue personal, professional, and social advantages. Deficient readers run higher risks of failure in all three areas.

- Nearly two-thirds of employers ranked reading comprehension "very important" for high school graduates. Yet 38 percent consider most high school graduates deficient in this basic skill.[6]

- American 15-year-olds ranked fifteenth in average reading scores for 31 industrialized nations, behind Poland, Korea, France, and Canada, among others.[7]

- Literary readers are more likely than nonreaders to engage in positive civic and individual activities, such as volunteering, attending sports or cultural events, and exercising.[8]

Notes

1. U.S. Department of Education, National Center for Education Statistics (NCES).

2. U.S. Department of Labor, Bureau of Labor Statistics, *American Time Use Survey* (2006).

3. U.S. Department of Education, NCES, *The Nation's Report Card: Reading 2005.*

4. U.S. Department of Education, NCES, *The Nation's Report Card: Reading 2005.*

5. U.S Department of Education, NCES, *National Assessment of Adult Literacy* (2007).

6. The Conference Board, *Are They Really Ready to Work?* (2006).

7. Organisation for Economic Co-operation and Development, *Learning for Tomorrow's World: First Results from PISA 2003.*

8. National Endowment for the Arts, *The Arts and Civic Engagement: Involved in Arts, Involved in Life* (2006).

Source: National Endowment for the Arts, *To Read or Not to Read.* http://www.nea.gov/news/news07/TRNR.html

American College Testing (ACT) shares college readiness benchmarks on its Web site (www.act.org). The high school profile for the graduating class of 2007 indicted that only 53 percent of the students met the readiness benchmark scores for reading. The National Average ACT reading score has gone from 21.3 in 1997 to 21.5 in 2007 with the years 2001 and 2002 dropping to 21.1 and 21.2, respectively.

From the Reach Out and Read National Center's "Reading Across the Nation: A Chartbook" report, written in October 2007, these were the key findings:

- Across the nation, just under half of children between birth and five years (47.8%) are read to every day by their parents or other family members.

- The percentage of families reading to their children every day varies by state and by race/ethnicity and family income within states.

- In virtually every state, minority and low-income children are less likely to be read to every day than their nonminority and higher-income peers.

- If a family member has some college education, 55 percent of children are read to every day, compared to 31 percent of children from families where no one completed high school.

- Only 30 percent of children from households in which the primary language is not English were read to daily compared with 51 percent in which the primary home language is English.

- The more words parents use when speaking to an eight-month-old infant, the greater the size of the child's vocabulary at age three.

The Problem: Children entering school not ready to learn

Up to one-third of American children enter kindergarten lacking at least some of the skills needed for a successful learning experience. For too many children, the preschool years have left them without the language skills necessary for literacy acquisition. When children are poor readers by the end of first grade, they are likely to remain so in fourth grade. Interventions in the early years that promote language development are powerful, cost-effective routes to improved school performance. The National Research Council's Committee on the Prevention of Reading Difficulties in Young Children stated that most reading difficulties can be prevented by promoting language and literacy development. (Snow, Burns, and Griffin, 1998)

The Solution: Parents reading aloud

Parents reading frequently to their children provides language and literacy skills that help children learn to read. Helping children to prepare for the challenge of learning to read before school entry is better than helping them catch up later. Reading aloud is the single most important activity for building the knowledge required for eventual success in reading. Early language skills, the foundation for later reading ability, are based primarily on language exposure and human interaction—parents and other adults talking to young children. The more words parents use when speaking to an eight-month-old infant, the greater the size of the child's vocabulary at age three. Many children from low-income families hear fewer words and learn fewer words, and their limited vocabularies essentially leave them language delayed at school entry, which places them at educational risk. Of all parent–child activities, reading aloud provides the richest exposure to language, so promotion of reading aloud, especially for children from more disadvantaged backgrounds, holds great promise for strengthening school readiness and laying a strong foundation for future educational success.

From Russ S, Perez V, Garro N, Klass P, Kuo AA, Gershun M, Halfon N, Zuckerman B. *Reading Across the Nation: A Chartbook* (2007): Reach Out and Read National Center, Boston, MA.
See http://www.reachoutandread.org/press_chart.html.

The National Institute for Literacy's report, "What Content Area Teachers Should Know About Adolescent Literacy" (October 2007) concludes:

> Countless middle and high school students at every socioeconomic level are struggling with learning academic content because they cannot read and write at grade level. To address this problem, all educators, including content-area teachers, need information on how to incorporate effective literacy learning strategies into the content-area curriculum.

Available at http://www.nifl.gov/nifl/publications/adolescent_literacy07.pdf.

Tweens and Teens Who Participate in Online Activities Are More Likely to Read Daily

New York, NY (June 11, 2008)—A new study released today finds that 75% of kids age 5–17 agree with the statement, "No matter what I can do online, I'll always want to read books printed on paper," and 62% of kids surveyed say they prefer to read books printed on paper rather than on a computer or a handheld device. The Kids & Family Reading Report™, a national survey of children age 5–17 and their parents, also found that kids who go online to extend the reading experience—by going to book or author websites or connecting with other readers—are more likely to read books for fun every day.

The 2008 Kids & Family Reading Report, a follow up to a similar 2006 study, both of which were conducted by Scholastic, the global children's publishing, education and media company, and TSC, a division of Yankelovich, a leader in consumer trends research, again found that the time kids spend reading books for fun declines after age eight and continues to drop off through the teen years.

"This year, we wanted to investigate the role technology plays in the drop-off in reading books for fun after age eight, and what we found surprised us," said Heather Carter, Director of Corporate Research, Scholastic. "Despite the fact that after age eight, more children go online daily than read for fun daily, high frequency Internet users are more likely to read books for fun every day. That suggests that parents and teachers can tap into kids' interest in going online to spark a greater interest in reading books."

The study also found that two-thirds of kids age 9-17 who go online have extended the reading experience via the Internet. These online reading extenders say they learn what other people think about a book, learn new things about an author and connect with other readers.

"Kids are very forward-thinking about ways technology can complement book reading," said Kristen Harmeling, Senior Researcher at Yankelovich. "They envision a time when most books are read digitally and when they can tag and share parts of books with other people online, making online reading a gateway to social activities; yet they still want printed books."

One in four kids age 5–17 say they read books for fun every day and more than half of kids say they read books for fun at least two to three times a week. One of the key reasons kids say they don't read more often is that they have trouble finding books they like – a challenge that parents underestimate. Kids who struggle to find books they like, are far less likely to read for fun daily or even twice a week.

The 2008 Kids & Family Reading Report also found that parents have a strong influence over kids' reading. They overwhelmingly view reading as the most important skill a child needs to develop, but only about half of all parents begin reading to their child before their first birthday. The percent of children who are read to every day drops from 38% among 5–8 year olds to 23% among 9–11 year olds. This is the same time that kids' daily reading for fun starts to decline.

"Parent engagement in their child's reading from birth all the way through the teen years can have a significant impact on how often their children read and how much they enjoy reading," added Carter.

A video presentation of the results from The Kids & Family Reading Report is available at www.scholastic.com/readingreport.

The following are additional key findings from the survey:

Kids and Reading:

- Kids overwhelmingly (89%) say, "My favorite books are the ones I picked out myself."
- Sixty-eight percent of kids say they love or like reading books for fun a lot (72% of girls/63% of boys).
- Half of all kids say there aren't enough really good books for boys/girls their age.

Technology and Reading:

- Both boys and girls (age 9–17) say that they prefer to read books rather than read things on the Internet when they want to use their imagination (63% vs. 37%).
- Boys are more likely to say the Internet is better than books when they want to read for fun (54% vs. 46%). Girls choose books (63% vs. 37%).
- Two in three children believe that within the next 10 years, most books which are read for fun will be read digitally—either on a computer or on another kind of electronic device.

Parents' Role:

- 82% of parents say they wish kids would read books for fun more often.
- Parents who read books for fun daily are six times more likely than low frequency reading parents to have kids who also read for fun daily.
- Parents are a key source of book suggestions for their children, but nearly half of all parents say they have a hard time finding information about books their child would enjoy reading, and especially parents of teens age 15–17 (62%).

Methodology:

The Kids and Family Reading Report is a national survey of 1002 individuals—501 children ages 5 to 17 years old and one parent or primary guardian per child. Interviews took place through mall-intercepts in 25 major cities across the country from January through February 2008. The survey was designed and analyzed by the staffs at Scholastic and Yankelovich. Quotas for gender and children's age were established to ensure ample base sizes for analysis purposes.

Source: http://www.scholastic.com/aboutscholastic/news/kfrr08web.pdf.

Kathleen Manzo (*Education Week,* May 7, 2008) reported that the interim report from the Reading First Impact Study stated that the $1 billion a year program had no measurable effect on students' reading comprehension. In August 13, 2008, Manzo reported that the What Works Clearinghouse stated that the two most widely used research-based reading programs failed to earn ratings. In the August/September 2008 issue of *Reading Today,* a publication of the International Reading Association, Stephen Krashen comments on the failure of Reading First. He brings out several issues that he says were not reported by the media.

Maria Glod of the *Washington Post* (November 19, 2008) reported that in a recent study by the U.S. Department of Education, students in the $6 billion Reading First program still are not scoring any better than students who were not in the program.

Cloues (2008) stated that the so-called research-based reading programs for Reading First are very strict about total devotion to leveled books (written with controlled vocabulary by the publishers of the reading programs) and are not allowed to use children's literature, which is placing "libraries last."

Krashen (2007) says that the key to reading success is access to an abundance of reading materials at school and at home. Krashen (2004) has also warned that the National Reading Panel made many false claims, and this is the report that started the planning for the Reading First program.

One thing is clear: there is much disagreement among the experts regarding reading instruction. After eight years and billions of dollars, the Reading First program is simply not working.

Annotated Resources

Krashen, Stephen. *The Power of Reading: Insights from the Research.* Libraries Unlimited, 2004.

Krashen, Emeritus Professor of Education at the University of Southern California, is the founder of free voluntary reading. This book covers free voluntary reading, direct instruction, benefits of reading, and reading and cognitive development.

McQuillan, J. *The Literacy Crisis: False Claims, Real Solutions.* Heinemann, 1998.

This book states that above all it is necessary to provide good books for kids. There are seven important points with regard to the literacy crisis as it was seen in 1998. Children are reading as well, if not better, than 25 years ago; scores are fairly stable over the same time period; dyslexia is not as rampant as once thought; there is a slight increase in reading test results over the past 50 years; U.S. students are good readers on a worldwide scale; scores are fairly stationary; and whole language did not undermine reading scores in California.

Neuman, S., Celano, D., Greco, A., & Shue, P. *Access for All: Closing the Book Gap for Children in Early Education.* International Reading Association, 2001.

This resource highlights the importance of providing books for all children starting at a very, very early age. It includes a national survey of access to books at early childhood centers and provides suggestions for how to get books into the hands of those who need them most.

Annotated Journal Articles

Allington, Richard L. "Setting the Record Straight." *Educational Leadership* (March 2004): 22–25.

Allington says that federal officials are holding schools to impossible standards based on misinterpretations of the research. He says that the interventions needed to ensure that *all* students will be reading on grade level have not been developed yet.

Cloues, Rachel. "Reading First, Libraries Last" (Spring 2008). Available at http://www.rethinkingschools.org.

Reading First, 2001, in which schools focus on a research-based reading program, means the exclusion of all other types of reading. Independent reading is gone, and in its place are leveled readers created from prescribed vocabulary. The school library is forgotten as children are directed to read only the books from the program.

Glod, Maria. "Study of Reading Program Finds a Lack of Progress." *Washington Post* (November 19, 2008): A06.

The final version of the study by the U.S. Department of Education regarding Reading First was released on November 18 and reported that children in the Reading First program did not perform better in reading comprehension than their peers who were not in the program.

Krashen, Stephen. "The Failure of Reading First." *Reading Today* (August/September 2008): 1.

> Writing about an Interim Report (April 30, 2008) about Reading First, Krashen states that the current dismal results are consistent with all previous reported outcomes. The Reading First program calls for a total of six extra weeks (an extra 10 minutes per day) of reading and even if the program and materials were a failure, the additional time spent should have had a positive impact.

Krashen, Stephen. "False Claims about Literacy Development." *Educational Leadership* (March 2004): 18–21.

> The National Reading Panel's conclusions are not proven facts. **False** claim #1: phonemic awareness training significantly improves reading ability. **False** claim #2: systematic phonics instruction is more effective than less systematic phonics instruction. **False** claim #3: skills-based approaches are superior to whole language approaches. **False** claim #4: there is no clear evidence that encouraging children to read more in school improves reading achievement.

Krashen, Stephen. "Literacy Campaigns: Access to Books is the First Step." *Literacy Network News* (Spring 2007): 7.

> More access to reading materials results in more reading. Books should be found in the home, in the classroom, and in the school library. It only takes a pleasant experience with a good book to increase enthusiasm in reading.

Manzo, Kathleen. "Studies of Popular Reading Texts Don't Make Grade." *Education Week* (August 13, 2008). Available at http://www/edweek.org/.

> The article states that two well-known research-based reading programs originally identified for the Reading First initiative have failed to earn ratings from the What Works Clearinghouse. Both Open Court and Reading Mastery did not satisfy the agency's rigorous evidence standards.

Manzo, Kathleen. "Reading First Doesn't Help Pupils 'Get It'—Other Factors Skewing Results of Study, Federal Officials Posit." *Education Week* (May 7, 2008). Available at http://www/edweek.org.

> The interim report on Reading First stated that the $1 billion a year program had no measurable effect on the reading comprehension of students.

Manzo, Kathleen. "Young People Seen Losing Love of Reading." *Education Week* (November 19, 2007). Available at http://www.edweek.org.

> Another article that discusses the fact that teens are reading less and that this is having an adverse affect on their reading test scores and other areas.

Motoko, Rich. "Study Links Drop in Test Scores to a Decline in Time Spent Reading" (November 19, 2007). Available at http://www.nytimes.com.

> It has been proven that reading for fun improves test scores. This article talks about the concerns of educators about middle and high school students who no longer read for fun and the adverse effect that this is having on test scores.

CHAPTER 2

Best Practices in Teaching Reading

Harvey Daniels, Steven Zemelman, Regie Routman, and Marie Carbo are a few experts who have shared lists of best practices in teaching reading. One of the most important factors is access to reading material. One cannot be successful at reading without actually having blocks of time to read and lots of great choices. Parental support through access to books at home from a very early age is an absolute necessity. Students need to have ample opportunities to discuss the books they read—with a reading partner, in small groups, and in the form of booktalks to their peers.

Learning to read is a strange phenomenon. Everyone knows of young children who seemingly taught themselves to read through constant exposure to lots of book and lots of people reading aloud to them. Some parents can teach their children to read by labeling things around the house and creating language experiences based on family events, trips, and life in general. Some learn quickly at school. Others struggle.

There are many ways to teach reading and many programs and tools are available. The most important point is: there is no one right way to teach children to read. It is important that the teacher has a full "bag of tricks" to provide the appropriate tools for success for each student. Once the basic decoding skills are taught and the child has a good solid sight-word vocabulary, the remaining years are spent fine-tuning.

Routman (2003) states that early and continual exposure to lots of books and oral language makes it easier for children to learn to read. Phonemic awareness does not need to be taught to the vast majority of beginning readers. Phonics instruction should be completed early in first grade and replaced by word analysis (contextual clues, syllable patterns, affixes). It is not necessary for all learners to be given a heavy dose of phonics; visual-spatial learners do far better learning to read using sight words and adding some analytic phonics later. Even for struggling readers, class time should be spent actually reading rather than doing worksheets and reading drills. Vocabulary development is extremely important, beginning with auditory vocabulary from being read to and talked to by adults from birth to building a vocabulary from abundant reading in all genres.

Opitz and Rasinski (1998) say that round-robin reading is not necessary. It can actually be harmful and embarrassing, and, most important, it tells the teacher nothing about reading skills—especially comprehension. If it is felt that reading aloud is necessary to check fluency, then students should be given time to practice or rehearse. Several excellent ways to check oral reading are readers' theater, paired reading, reading with recorded text, and choral reading.

Altwerger (2007) says that No Child Left Behind and Reading First have required teachers to spend a great deal of time improving oral reading. As a result, fluency has taken a very important place in the teaching of reading. This has put silent and independent reading further down the list and actually caused them to be neglected. She further states that fluency is not the cornerstone of reading. Reading fluently and accurately does not necessarily mean successful comprehension. The most important thing should be understanding text.

Allington (2009) has written a book all about fluency. The National Reading Panel pointed to fluency as being a very important factor in learning to read. As a result, fluency programs such as DIBELS took on a new life. According to Allington, DIBELS is not a fluency assessment. His book offers suggestions as to why children have fluency issues and what to do about them.

Hearing books read aloud is the beginning of learning to read. Allington (2001) claims that it is very important to provide kids with access to an abundance of books. The selection should include a wide variety of genres, and the books should be comfortable for the children to read. There should be a rotating classroom library collection so that readers have the opportunity to select from a regularly changing variety of titles that are always at hand. It is so important to have access to many books in the classroom that instead of purchasing a basal reader and workbooks, those dollars would be better spent on novels and picture books for the classroom.

Reading can develop and extend interests based on prior knowledge. It is important to collaborate with your librarian/media specialist for connections to specific books for children with certain interests. It is also important to introduce students to authors and illustrators. Reading about how an author began writing, their likes and dislikes, if the characters in the story are based on real people, and other similar information makes the experience real and personal. The teacher should initiate contact with the author of a class favorite. It is amazing to get an e-mail or a letter back from an author. Many do respond.

Best practices in teaching reading comprehension are highlighted by Brassell and Rasinski (2008). Understanding text is the underpinning of a successful reading program. They discuss seven types of comprehension instruction: graphic organizers, semantic organizers, question answering and generation, text structure, summarization, cooperative learning, and comprehension monitoring. Comprehension takes place when students are engaged in reading. Background knowledge is critical in effective comprehension instruction.

Ivey and Fisher (2005) suggest that teachers should let students read rather than spend time doing skill worksheets and note how important it is to allow young readers to select what interests them. It is important not to interrogate students about their reading but instead to give them open-ended questions to facilitate lively discussions with their peers about their reading.

Jalongo (2004) asks the question, why should we read aloud to children who can read independently? She shares seven reasons: to foster appreciation, extend background knowledge and interest, expand preferences, develop listening comprehension, model what good readers do, share literature responses, and entertain and encourage development in language arts.

Gambrell (2007) talks about how necessary practice is to becoming a good reader and strongly suggests the effort needed to organize independent reading as part of the school day. It demonstrates how essential reading is if you make time during the day to pleasure read.

Juel and Deffes (2004) have advice about teaching vocabulary. They say it is important to develop vocabulary to the fullest extent in the early years. Teachers should provide clear explanations and give repeated occasions for students to hear words in context. Making connections to background knowledge and prior learning is important. Gone are the days of looking up words and writing and memorizing definitions.

From the earliest school grades, reading should be linked to the content areas so that the students see the connection. Both fiction and nonfiction titles should be used in the content areas. Students should have ample opportunity to discuss what they have read with their peers and to recommend titles that they enjoyed.

Annotated Resources

Allington, Richard. *What Really Matters for Struggling Readers: Designing Research-Based Programs.* Longman, 2001.

Allington discusses reading instruction in American schools. What really matters is that kids need to read a lot, and they need access to books they can read comfortably. The book provides information on providing appropriate instruction for struggling readers.

Allington, Richard. *What Really Matters in Fluency: Research-Based Practices across the Curriculum.* Pearson, 2009.

Allington discusses the meaning of fluency and why it is such a hot topic, how it is developed normally, how to assess it, and how to develop it in struggling readers.

Altwerger, Bess, Nancy Jordan, & Nancy Shelton. *Rereading Fluency: Process, Practice, and Policy.* Heinemann, 2007.

Allington provides the forward in this book about fluency. It provides a new look at fluency—the relationship between fluency and comprehension and phonics versus literature programs. It answers the questions, can fluency measure the difference between more and less proficient readers? Should fluency be considered a critical component of reading?

Brassell, Danny, & Timothy Rasinski. *Comprehension That Works: Taking Students beyond Ordinary Understanding to Deep Comprehension.* Shell Education, 2008.

Brassell and Rasinski discuss engaging student interest, what proficient readers do, identifying difficulties with comprehension, differentiating instruction, and comprehension strategies.

Cunningham, Patricia, & Richard Allington. *Classrooms That Work: They Can All Read and Write.* Addison-Wesley Longman, 1999.

This book provides great strategies for teaching reading. It covers developing decoding and spelling fluency; strategies for reading in science and social studies; guiding children's reading and writing; actual lessons from kindergarten, primary, and intermediate classrooms; and reading beyond the classroom.

Daniels, Harvey, & Marilyn Bizar. *Teaching the Best Practice Way, Methods That Matter, K–12.* Stenhouse Publishers, 2005.

Best practice resources are always important to review. This one includes reading as thinking, publishing and creating, small-group work, classroom workshops, authentic experiences, reflective assessment, and integrative units.

Jalongo, Mary. *Young Children and Picture Books.* National Association for the Education of Young Children, 2004.

> This book focuses on the question, why read aloud to children who can read independently? According to Jalongo there are seven reasons: to foster appreciation, extend background and interest, expand preferences, develop listening comprehension, model what good readers do, share literature responses, and entertain and encourage child development in language arts.

Marzano, Robert, Debra Pickering, & Jane Pollack. *Classroom Instruction That Works: Research-Based Strategies for Increasing Student Achievement.* Association for Supervision and Curriculum Development, 2001.

> Marzano and coauthors provide information on research-based strategies for teaching including similarities, differences, summarizing, note taking, homework, generating and testing hypotheses, and specific applications.

Opitz, M., & T. Rasinski. *Good-Bye Round Robin.* Heinemann, 1998.

> This title provides information about the potentially harmful effects of round-robin reading on students who are struggling readers. It provides many great suggestions for safe reading aloud with practice time beforehand.

Reutzel, D. R., & R. B. Cooter. *Teaching Children to Read: From Basals to Books.* Merrill, 1996.

> This was one of my favorite texts for teaching reading to college students working on an elementary education degree. It describes three methods for teaching reading and states that no single method works; sometimes parts of all three are necessary. The three methods are decoding (or phonics), skills, and balanced. The skills method includes letters and sounds, sight words, and story structure. The balanced method includes whole language, read-alouds, independent reading, authentic writing, and themes.

Routman, Regie. *Reading Essentials: The Specifics You Need to Teach Reading Well.* Heinemann, 2003.

> This is an excellent resource for all those interested in developing lifelong readers. It includes information on bonding with students, stressing that there is no one way or right way to teach reading, ideas for excellent teaching of reading, creating an excellent classroom library, building an independent reading program for all students, using reading programs as resources, and managing your time.

Zemelman, Steven, Harvey Daniels, & Arthur Hyde. *Best Practice: New Standards for Teaching and Learning in America's Schools.* Heinemann, 1998.

> This resource covers all school disciplines, but the section on best practices in teaching reading is especially important and timeless. It reviews an exemplary program, discusses the reading wars, lists the National Council of Teachers of English standards for language arts, and describes 14 best practices for teaching reading. It concludes with ways that parents and school principals can help.

Annotated Journal Articles

Adler, C. R. "Seven Strategies to Teach Students Reading Comprehension." *Reading Rockets.* Available at http://www.readingrockets.org

> The strategies are as follows: monitoring comprehension, metacognition, graphic and semantic organizers, answering questions, generating questions, recognizing story structure, and summarizing.

Allington, Richard. "The Other Five 'Pillars' of Effective Reading Instruction." *Reading Today* (June 2005): 3.

> The National Reading Panel listed five pillars for reading instruction: phonological awareness, phonics, fluency, vocabulary, and comprehension. In this article, Allington adds five more "pillars" of reading instruction. These include classroom organization, matching pupils and texts, access to interesting texts, choice and collaboration, and expert tutoring.

Biancarosa, Gina. "After Third Grade." *Educational Leadership* (October 2005): 16–22.

> Instructional strategies that will help students gain new knowledge after third grade are described, including direct comprehension instruction, instruction embedded in content, motivation, self-directed learning, collaborative learning, strategic tutoring, diverse text, intensive writing, technology, and ongoing formative assessment.

Duke, Nell. "The Case for Informational Text." *Educational Leadership* (March 2004): 40–44.

> Younger students need to be exposed to regular doses of informational texts. Increase access and increase time for them to read and explore interesting topics. Teach comprehension strategies for informational texts. Use informational texts for authentic purposes—reading for writing.

Gambrell, Linda. "Reading: Does Practice Make Perfect?" *Reading Today* (June/July 2007): 16.

> Practice helps students become better readers. The productive use of independent reading time during the school day is critical to the development of both the skill and the will to read. Independent reading time does require teacher attention and monitoring, but it is well worth the effort.

Grimes, Sharon. "The Search for Meaning: How You Can Boost Kids' Reading Comprehension." *School Library Journal* (May 2004): 48–52.

> This article provides a useful reading checklist and five steps to creating a schoolwide program. Build a learning community for students and staff. Provide direct instruction in reading strategies of proficient readers. Design ways that students can independently use comprehension skills. Teach teachers how to collect and analyze data to monitor and modify instruction. Celebrate and share success.

Ivey, Gay, & Douglas Fisher. "Learning from What Doesn't Work." *Educational Leadership* (October 2005): 8–14.

> Strategies that work: letting kids read rather than do worksheets on skills, allow students to read what interests them, teach students to find "just right" books so they read at their comfort level, do not interrogate students about their reading, don't stick them in front of a computer program that will supposedly help them learn to read.

Juel, Connie, & Rebecca Deffes. "Making Words Stick." *Educational Leadership* (March 2004): 30–34.

> Focus on words contextualized in literature, provide clear explanations, and give repeated occasions for students to hear words in context. Other ways to develop vocabulary are through background knowledge and by looking closely at word structure. Using whatever works, it is important to develop students' vocabulary to the fullest extent in the early grades.

Katch, Jane. "The Most Important Words." *Educational Leadership* (March 2004): 62–64.

> Lists of "special" words can spark preschoolers' interest in reading. Create a word wall list for each student and add meaningful words that are part of each student's daily discussion and interest.

Scharer, Patricia, Gay Su Pinnell, Carol Lyons, and & Irene Fountas. "Becoming an Engaged Reader." *Educational Leadership* (October 2005): 24–29.

    Effective readers think within the text, beyond the text, and about the text. Interactive read-alouds and literature discussions are ways for students to expand their vocabulary and understanding of text. Classroom libraries are important. There should be an emotional connection with reading.

Schroder, Monika. "Reading Is Thinking: Modeling Comprehension Strategies with Picture Books." *Book Links* (May 2008): 56–59.

    This article uses a variety of picture books to help struggling readers with comprehension. The picture books are described, and there are suggestions for connections.

Strickland, Dorothy. "Laying the Literacy Groundwork." *Educational Leadership* (March 2004): 74–77.

    Oral language is most important. Alphabetic knowledge is also key. Print-rich environments finish out the perfect picture.

CHAPTER 3

Best Practices in Teaching Reading to Adolescents

Content area teachers in middle and high school must provide their students with strategies for dealing with challenging texts, unfamiliar material, and important information using a variety of sources. When content area texts are evaluated using a readability level test, it is understandable why many students have difficulty comprehending the content and vocabulary. Even middle and high school students who are proficient in math can have difficulty with math tests given inaccurate reading of word problems and directions.

All teachers and media specialists need to understand that reading aloud to students should not stop at third grade—it should continue into the high school years. Follos (2007) emphasizes the importance of reading aloud to teens. Taking time out of a precious class period to share a good book demonstrates the value and importance of reading.

Moses (2008) talks about the importance of literature circles and clearly describes the value of the student conversations that result. She cautions that the teacher should not dominate or even participate in the discussion. Johnson and Freedman (2005) focus on literature circles solely in content areas in which comfortable book discussion and enjoyable reading in a content area are not usually the norm. Robb (2003) even provides valuable lists of content-area-related children's literature titles. Finally, Billman (2002) discusses the effective use of picture books for older students in content area classes. She provides lists of titles organized by topic.

Vacca (2002) insists that teachers should teach both reading and writing strategies as associated to content area texts. Angelillo (2003) states that to validate the importance of the reading–writing connection, a reading log is essential not only for keeping a record of titles read but also for reflections about each reading experience.

Normal focus for content area reading according to Daniels and Zemelman (2003/2004) is on the text and perhaps some primary documents. The text should be used only as a reference (like an encyclopedia or dictionary) because most texts for content area courses are difficult to read and cover a tremendous amount of material in a few pages. Reading in content areas should include historical and science fiction, picture books, and nonfiction titles. Part of class time should be spent in book discussion groups or literature circles as a way to enhance and share additional information and concepts on a specific topic within the discipline.

Tovani (2004) relates that it is important to assist middle and upper school content area teachers in helping their students with reading skills. Content area teachers realize that they are not specifically trained to teach reading, but they also know how important being a good reader is to content area success. It is also important for content area teachers to value their students' prior learning to make good connections to the new material they are teaching.

Borzo and Flynt (2008) share six evidence-based principles for increasing motivation in content area classrooms: boost academic self-efficacy, spark interest in content, connect school to the outside world, provide access to interesting texts, expand choices and options, and maximize collaboration and teamwork.

The amount of vocabulary introduced in some content areas, especially in high school, is staggering. It is extremely important that all content area teachers know how to teach vocabulary effectively. Fisher, Frey, and Lapp (2008) remind teachers that vocabulary words should be introduced by connecting them with background knowledge. In fact, the only way they can be remembered is through a pathway connecting them to knowledge that is already there. To make the new words permanent, they must be used. The teacher should model their use in speaking and writing and ask the students to do the same. Most students will need to memorize the words using flash cards—some will need to add an illustration to help them remember. Words and meanings can be chanted, sung, or made into acronyms. Hinchman and Sheridan-Thomas (2008) talk further about the role of vocabulary and suggest that it influences comprehension, improves general achievement, enhances thinking and communication, and promotes fluency.

Coiro (2005) reminds teachers that students today are heavily grounded in technology. Therefore, it is important for them to make meaningful connections with Internet texts. They must be able to follow links confidently, decide on the best search engines, and then determine whether the information they find is true. Often they can discover page after page of information on a topic, but they must recognize that the content must be read and sorted; of course the most difficult part is how to synthesize the information without copying. Copying and pasting is so easy to do. Students should be allowed to blog and create Web pages and videos to demonstrate understanding of a concept.

Sustained silent reading is another important topic that needs to be addressed and valued in the middle and upper grades in content area classes. Teachers must be involved in encouraging their students to read independently. They can read aloud the beginning chapter of a related fiction or nonfiction book from the library and ask who would like to find out what happens and then give the book to that student to read and share his or her reaction with peers at a later time. They also need to share author information with students. Very often, authors are accessible and will respond to e-mails; publishing houses will send author kits for classroom or library displays as well.

During a middle school book club breakfast, I was discussing *Yankee Girl* (Rodman, Mary Ann; Farrar, Straus & Giroux, 2004) with a group of middle school girls who had read the book. They enjoyed it and wondered aloud if there might be a sequel coming. When I returned to my office, I looked up the author, went to her Web site, found her e-mail address, then sent her an e-mail. I explained what had just transpired and asked the question. She must have been online because I got an e-mail back almost immediately. She was thrilled that I had written, had been pondering a sequel, and because of these girls' interest, decided she would go ahead with the project! I immediately forwarded the e-mail to the literature teacher to share with the girls. They were very excited.

Gardiner (2007) lists the areas of improvement from independent reading—vocabulary, comprehension, and comfort with reading. He tells how important classroom libraries are so that students are never far from a good book if the opportunity to read presents itself. Humphrey and Preddy

(2008) claim that sustained silent reading is necessary for reading practice and share ideas for starting and sustaining schoolwide programs.

Annotated Resources

Allen, Janet. *Words, Words, Words: Teaching Vocabulary in Grades 4–12.* Stenhouse Publishers, 1999.
> This is a wonderful tool for teaching vocabulary with topics that include a vocabulary-rich classroom, word control, using context, and alternatives to "look it up in the dictionary!"

Angelillo, Janet. *Writing about Reading—From Book Talk to Literary Essays, Grades 3–8.* Heinemann, 2003.
> This resource discusses thinking and talking about texts, using a reader's notebook, various genres, the literary essay, writing and reading in the content areas, evaluating written work, transforming students into lifelong readers.

Hinchman, Kathleen, & Heather Sheridan-Thomas (eds.). *Best Practices in Adolescent Literacy Instruction,* Guilford Press, 2008.
> This resource includes nineteen essays from important researchers in the field of adolescent literacy. The essays are organized into three categories: perspectives toward adolescent literacy instruction, developing reading and writing strategies for multiple contexts, and adolescent literacy program issues.

Jacobs, Heidi Hayes. *Active Literacy across the Curriculum: Strategies for Reading, Writing, Speaking, and Listening.* Eye on Education, 2006.
> Jacobs provides information on every teacher becoming an active language teacher. She shares tips on teaching ESOL students, note taking, editing, revising, speaking, listening, and revising. She also discusses the importance and use of integrating curriculum maps in grades K–12.

Johnson, Holly, & Lauren Freedman. *Content Area Literature Circles: Using Discussion for Learning across the Curriculum.* Christopher-Gordon Publishers, 2005.
> This book is a great resource for creating a climate of comfortable book discussion in the content area classrooms where it is very important to make the connection between reading and those disciplines not normally associated with reading and discussion.

McKenna, Michael. *Help for Struggling Readers: Strategies for Grades 3–8.* The Guilford Press, 2008.
> Strategies for struggling readers include decoding, fluency, vocabulary, comprehension, and questioning.

Nichols, Maria. *Talking about Text: Guiding Students to Increase Comprehension through Purposeful Talk.* Shell Education, 2008.
> This resource provides information on the changing role of the classroom teacher, teaching purposeful talk behavior, and creating habits of mind that encourage students to read, think, and talk independently.

Robb, Laura. *Teaching Reading in Social Studies, Science, and Math: Practical Ways to Weave Comprehension Strategies into Your Content Area Teaching.* Scholastic, 2003.
> Robb provides the reader with a whole new approach to content area reading. The book is filled with strategies to use before, during, and after learning and to help with scaffolding instruction. It also focuses on using discussion effectively (including sample prompts), exploring textbook structures, new ways to look at teaching vocabulary, and how to focus on content area related children's literature titles.

Robb, Laura. *Teaching Reading in the Middle School: A Strategic Approach to Teaching Reading that Improves Comprehension and Thinking.* Scholastic, 2000.

> This book lists some ways to support struggling readers in the middle school classroom. Teachers should be positive, set reasonable goals for students, get students actively involved in their learning, and try using different strategies when the usual ones aren't working. The teacher should be prepared to work one-on-one for extra explanations when other things aren't working. Students should be given extra time to process, they should be given opportunities to retell information in small groups, and it is important to make sure that the students understand all directions. Some struggling readers should have the help of a reading specialist, then they should regularly reflect on their progress.

Tovani, Cris. *Do I Really Have to Teach Reading? Content Comprehension, Grades 6–12.* Stenhouse Publishers, 2004.

> It has been proven that content area teachers must also be reading teachers. This reference provides strategies for all middle and high school teachers realizing that they are not specifically trained to teach reading but that they also know how important being a good reader is to content area success. Topics include comprehension, note taking, group work, and assessment.

Annotated Journal Articles

Barton, Mary Lee, Clare Heidema, & Deborah Jordan. "Teaching Reading in Mathematics and Science." *Educational Leadership* (November 2002): 24–28.

> Content area science and math teachers must first activate their students' prior knowledge, even if it is poor. Teachers need to assist students in strengthening any and all connections to prior learning. They must assist students in mastering content area vocabulary (a high school chemistry text can have as many as 3,000 new terms). They must also help students to understand the specific style of the text they are using.

Bean, Thomas W. "Making Reading Relevant for Adolescents." *Educational Leadership* (November 2002): 34–37.

> Abundant independent reading can make a huge difference for adolescent readers. Teachers must help students find books that connect with the curriculum for students to read comfortably, learn from, and enjoy. It is very important to connect adolescents with all kinds of good books.

Billman, Linda Webb. "Aren't These Books for Little Kids?" *Educational Leadership* (November 2002): 48–51.

> There are many great picture books that connect middle school students with historical events and people. This article provides a list of picture book titles suitable for middle school students and organized by topic.

Borzo, William, & Sutton Flynt. "Motivating Students to Read in the Content Classroom: Six Evidence-Based Principles." *The Reading Teacher* (October 2008): 172–174.

> Here are the authors' six evidence-based principles for increasing motivation: boost academic self-efficacy, spark interest in content, connect school to the outside world, give students access to interesting texts, expand choices and options, and maximize collaboration.

Chehayl, Laurel. "Books in Action!" *Middle School Journal* (September 2008): 26–32.

> This article describes an independent-reading project for middle school students. One book project is to be completed within a nine-week timeframe, but the length of time can be flexible. There

are project options with varying point values, and students can select what they want to do to achieve the grade they want. The article gives many excellent project ideas.

Coiro, Julie. "Making Sense of Online Text." *Educational Leadership* (October 2005): 30–35.

Coiro provides strategies for adolescents to use to make meaningful connections with Internet texts. This is a new kind of literacy – following links, web site navigation, deciding what is true information, and how to synthesize without copying.

Coutant, Carolyn, & Natalia Perchemlides. "Strategies for Teen Readers." *Educational Leadership* (October 2005): 42–47.

Genre-specific reading strategies are helpful for teen readers. This article includes strategies for working with expository and narrative texts.

Daniels, Harvey, & Steven Zemelman. "Out with the Textbooks, In with Learning." *Educational Leadership* (December 2003/January 2004): 36–40.

Textbooks should be viewed as reference materials and used when needed. Texts should be thought of in the same category as encyclopedias, dictionaries, and thesauruses. Many texts are really unreadable, and many take a very superficial look at a very broad topic. Teachers should work toward a balanced diet of reading in the content areas with a variety of authentic nonfiction and even some novels.

D'Arcangelo, Marcia. "The Challenge of Content-Area Reading: A Conversation with Donna Ogle." *Educational Leadership* (November 2002): 12–15.

Many middle and high school teachers think of themselves as content experts. Content area teachers need to incorporate reading strategies into their content lessons. Students in middle and high school today lack these basic skills because they have not chosen to read independently to practice.

Fisher, Douglas, Nancy Frey, & Diane Lapp. "Shared Readings: Modeling Comprehension, Vocabulary, Text Structures, and Text Features for Older Readers." *The Reading Teacher* (April 2008): 548–556.

This article tells about the modeling practices of good reading teachers. During shared reading, they model strategies for comprehension and vocabulary. They also model strategies for text structures (compare/contrast, problem/solution, cause/effect, and story grammar) and text features (headings, captions, illustrations, charts, tables, diagrams, glossaries, and graphs).

Follos, Alison. "Change the Literacy Depression in Your School: Read Teens a Story!" *Library Media Connection* (April/May 2007): 20–22.

Reading aloud to teens is important—it can be part of a book club, a literature circle, or just for literature appreciation. It is important to give students choice and lots of great titles from which to choose. Then it is necessary to give them the time to read. Readers' workshop is an important activity for these students, and it often leads to a big change in their attitudes toward reading.

Gardiner, Steve. "Librarians Provide Strongest Support for Sustained Silent Reading." *Library Media Connection* (February 2007): 16–18.

Every day. Every class period. That is how sustained silent reading works best. Series books are always popular, but in a high school setting, there needs to be a wide variety of selections to provide books for the wide span of reading tastes between freshmen and seniors. Classroom libraries are extremely important, and this article refers to the Read It Forward Web site (http://senior. billings.k12.mt.us/readitforward/index.php), which encourages everyone—students, teachers, administrators, parents, and support staff—to read a good book and share their enthusiasm for it with others.

Gardiner, Steve. "A Skill for Life." *Educational Leadership* (October 2005): 67–70.

Sustained silent reading can improve vocabulary, comprehension, and reading motivation. Attributes of good readers include the following: sometimes reading more than one book at one time, rereading part or all of a book, taking a book along wherever you go, stop reading a book you do not like, share reading reactions with others, and enjoy the freedom of book selection.

Guensbburg, Carol. "Reading Rules: The Word of the Day Is 'Literacy.' " Edutopia Web site (February 1, 2006). Available at http://www.edutopia.org/reading-rules.

Reading across the curriculum takes on new meaning in this high school in Falls Church, Virginia. All freshmen take a required literacy course because it is a low-income community and two-thirds of the students speak English as a second language. Absenteeism was rampant, and three-fourths of the students read at least two years below grade level. All teachers, regardless of their subject, were trained to teach reading, and literacy became a focus every day in every class. As a result of this effort, things have been completely turned around at this high school.

Humphrey, Jack, & Leslie Preddy. "Keys to Successfully Sustaining an SSR Program." *Library Media Connection* (March 2008): 30–32.

Young adolescents need to keep reading skills sharp with lots of practice. A silent sustained reading (SSR) program will do just that. It is important to get the administration to endorse the SSR program, and you need an SSR/Literacy Committee to implement the program, provide staff and student training, and develop promotions and projects. Each classroom must have a classroom library that changes frequently and is always well stocked with great titles. Time needs to be created within the daily schedule, the media center needs to take an active part, and the school must believe in and support a culture of reading.

Ivey, Gay, & Marianne Baker. "Phonics Instruction for Older Students/Just Say No." *Educational Leadership* (March 2004): 35–39.

There is no case for phonics instruction in the intermediate grades and beyond. Use the right books—texts that kids can and want to read. Explore words within real reading and writing. Help students make sense of their reading—these students need good teachers.

Ivey, Gay, & Douglas Fisher. "When Thinking Skills Trump Reading Skills." *Educational Leadership* (October 2006): 16–21.

Back to basics programs and adolescents are not a good mix. Use accessible texts with rich concepts, use alternative texts to spur critical reading, use read-alouds and think-alouds, and use writing to tap critical knowledge.

Jacobs, Vicki. "Reading, Writing, and Understanding." *Educational Leadership* (November 2002): 58–61.

Secondary school teachers think of themselves as content area experts, not reading teachers. This attitude can change if they see how reading and writing to learn strategies help students to understand content area texts.

McConachie, Stephanie, Megan Hall, Lauren Resnick, Anita K. Ravi, Victoria L. Bill, Jody Bintz, & Joseph A. Taylor. "Task, Text, and Talk Literacy for All Subjects." *Educational Leadership* (October 2006): 8–14.

> Knowing and thinking must go hand in hand. Learning is apprenticeship. Teachers must mentor students. Instruction and assessment drive each other. Classroom culture socializes intelligence.

Moses, Alexandra R. "Reading Round Table: Literature Circles Expand Thought." Edutopia Web site (February 26, 2008). Available at http://www.edutopia.org/literature-circles.

> This article provides another look at literature circles, with the focus on differences—no two circles are the same. The emphasis should be on the students' conversation. Offer students a choice, teachers should not dominate or even participate in any discussion, generic discussion prompts should be provided, and students should be encouraged to reflect on the literature circle experience.

Salinger, Terry, & Steve Fleischman. "Teaching Students to Interact with Text." *Educational Leadership* (October 2005): 90–92.

> Secondary teachers can make a difference; this article focuses only on the strategy of questioning the author. Teachers need to help students synthesize, analyze, and integrate new ideas into content area reading.

Tovani, Cris. "The Power of Purposeful Reading." *Educational Leadership* (October 2005): 48–51.

> Teachers must make the purpose of reading very clear to help content area adolescent readers with challenging texts. They must help students be selfish readers, to reread with new purpose, and to read to connect.

Vacca, Richard. T. "From Efficient Decoders to Strategic Readers." *Educational Leadership* (November 2002): 6–11.

> Vacca discusses the importance of helping adolescent learners use reading and writing strategies to learn with texts. All content area teachers must be aware of this critical need.

CHAPTER 4

Brain Research and Reading

Brain imaging techniques are becoming more sophisticated and revealing more about the function of the brain. Scientists are discovering new things about the current meaning of developmentally appropriate and what activities and processes are brain-friendly. Experts in the field are then taking that information and translating it into useful classroom activities and practices.

Beginning with general ideas about how the brain works most effectively, Jensen (1998) tells us that the brain functions best with lots of feedback and when learning is connected to emotions. He recommends using mind mapping as an organization tool because that is the way the brain works—not linearly but in networks. He says we need to affirm and celebrate our learning and have downtime to reflect on our learning. Connecting to prior knowledge is necessary to cement current learning. Finally, a stimulating working environment is a must.

Speaking is a natural process, but reading is not, according to Sousa (2005). Eventually, however, most of us learn the process of decoding the printed word, one way or another, and this process becomes automatic.

It is known that even students with high intelligence have to work to succeed. Brain power does not immediately translate to success without determination and effort. Struggling is good for the brain, according to Dweck (2008).

King-Friedrichs (2001) relates the importance of using brain-friendly techniques when teaching reading. Connecting to prior knowledge and personal relevance are two of the most important factors in helping students to remember lessons and strategies.

All agree that both developing and sharing language at an early age and being read to from as early as six months are extremely important. The foundation for literacy is set early in life. Barlow (1997) states that early exposure to books and language is the key to school and reading success. Those most adversely affected are those who are at or below the poverty level and do not utilize libraries.

Brain research has proven, according to Sprenger (2002), that students need many reading choices and opportunities to discuss their reading in an informal way; they also need challenging activities and ample feedback from their teachers.

Wolfe (2004) states that the primary years are the best for teaching children to read because that is when the brain is most plastic and malleable and therefore ready to learn. She also agrees that mind mapping is a better organization tool than a linear list because that is the way the brain processes information—through neural networks or circuits. She says there is no such thing as students not paying attention; the brain is always paying attention to something. Wolfe states that it is necessary to understand memory systems to comprehend the reading process and that automaticity in reading is only the result of abundant practice. She also tells us that a good predictor of future reading success is how quickly and well a child learns the alphabet and how important hearing and repeating nursery rhymes, poems, and chants are to the prereading process.

Tate (2003) tells us that important strategies for growing dendrites include questioning, discussion, drawing and illustrating, graphic organizers, mind maps, and webs for understanding, group discussion, drama, storytelling, writing, and journaling.

Sprenger (2005) says that there are ways to reach sleep-deprived adolescent learners so they can actually learn during early-morning classes. They need lively discussion with peers, role-playing and creating artwork in groups, and making emotional connections with what they are reading.

Furr (2000) shared a specific neurological impress method for teaching reading. He listed explicit step-by-step instructions to focus on perceptual, syntactic, and semantic processes, word recognition, and comprehension. Not much has been written recently about this method and its success rate.

We know that the research continues regarding how the brain learns best and what we can do with that information to help more students have success with the process of learning to read.

Annotated Resources

Fogarty, Robin. *Literacy Matters: Strategies Every Teacher Can Use*. Corwin Press, 2007.

> Fogarty provides a number of easy-to-use strategies for approaching literacy. The text includes learning to learn with metacognitive reflections, seven strategies for teaching comprehension, using prior knowledge to support schema theory, using brain and learning principles, reading attitude matters, intervention strategies, teaching vocabulary using technology, read aloud, multiple intelligences, and guided reading.

Furr, David. *Reading Clinic: A New Way to Teach Reading (Brain Research Applied to Reading)*. Truman House, 2000.

> This book demonstrates a new method for teaching reading using brain research. It is called the neuro-reading method. The method includes perceptual, syntactic, and semantic processes, word recognition, and comprehension. There are step-by-step lessons and appendices filled with helpful information.

Jensen, Eric. *Teaching with the Brain in Mind*. Association for Supervision and Curriculum Development, 1998.

> This is a practical guide to using brain research in the classroom. It covers all aspects of learning but includes some important messages about teaching reading. Jensen states that children should be read to starting at six months of age. Challenging vocabulary is best learned before twelve years of age. In most cases, it is better to teach sight words before phonics (whole before parts).

Perez, Kathy. *More than 100 Brain-Friendly Tools and Strategies for Literacy Instruction*. Corwin Press, 2008.

> This book is a wonderful resource for brain-friendly activities. It includes puzzles, strategies, classroom management tips, many examples of differentiation, and basic instructional strategies.

Sousa, David A. *How the Brain Learns to Read*. Corwin Press, 2005.

Sousa begins with a discussion of the process of learning spoken language and the various levels of language comprehension. Learning to read is not a natural ability, and Sousa discusses early stages of learning to read, comprehension, memory, and the importance of practice. Next he shares information about the teaching of reading, modern methods, and research findings. There are two chapters on recognizing and overcoming reading problems. There is also a section about the importance of content area reading and how important it is to make a good effort to close the reading achievement gap.

Sprenger, Marilee. *Becoming a "Wiz" at Brain-Based Teaching: How to Make Every Year Your Best Year*. Corwin Press, 2002.

Students need choices and to have opportunities to work together and discuss outcomes. They need to journal about reading. They need challenging activities and lots of teacher feedback.

Tate, Marcia. *Worksheets Don't Grow Dendrites: 20 Instructional Strategies That Engage the Brain*. Corwin Press, 2003.

Some of the important strategies include questioning, discussion, drawing and illustrating, graphic organizers, mind maps, and webs for understanding, group discussion, drama, storytelling, writing, and journaling.

Wolfe, Patricia, & Pamela Nevills. *Building the Reading Brain, PreK–3*. Corwin Press & Sage Publications, 2004.

Beginning with the nature of reading, this resource includes informative sections on what happens to the brain when children read, breaking the reading code, comprehension and vocabulary, and helping at-risk readers.

Annotated Journal Articles

Barlow, Carla. "Ooooh Baby, What a Brain!" *School Library Journal* (July 1997): 20–22.

It has been proven that lots of early exposure to books and language is the key to school and reading success. Those most adversely affected are those who are at or below the poverty level and do not utilize libraries. In some cases, parents themselves might not be able to read. More and more organizations are trying to bring books to all babies, but mostly to those at the poverty level.

Bower, Bruce." Learning to Read Evokes Hemispheric Trade-off." *Science News* (May 24, 2004): 324.

New research has discovered that certain reading tasks—relationships between sounds and letters—take place in the left hemisphere, and the right hemisphere supplies the brain with word-related visual knowledge.

Bower, Bruce. "Read All about It: Kids Take Different Neural Paths to Reach Print Mastery." *Science News* (April 30, 2005): 280.

Recent research has shown that many different parts of reading take place in different areas of the brain.

Dweck, Carol. "Brainology: Transforming Students' Motivation to Learn." *Independent School* (Winter 2008): 110–119.

It is very important to let students know that no one has a gift that guarantees success. Everyone, regardless of their gift, has to add enormous amounts of dedication and effort to be successful. It is through effort that people build their abilities and realize their potential. It is meaningful to struggle with something and make progress. That is what makes us smarter.

King-Friedrichs, Jeanne. "Brain-Friendly Techniques for Improving Memory." *Educational Leadership* (November 2001): 76–79.

    Connect to prior knowledge, develop personal relevance, elaborate on key concepts, rehearse retrieval clues, use a variety of assessments, and remember that learning must be connected to what students already know.

Sprenger, Marilee. "Inside Amy's Brain." *Educational Leadership* (April 2005): 28–32.

    Sprenger provides teaching tips so that sleep-deprived adolescent learners can actually learn during early-morning classes. She also provides excellent information about adolescent brain development.

Willis, Judy. "The Gully in the Brain Glitch Theory." *Educational Leadership* (February 2007): 68–73.

    New advances in neuroscience support reading enjoyment more than intensive phonics. Reading is not an isolated process; it is a complex one that connects centers in the brain. A phonics-embedded approach that uses literature to teach reading skills and strategies is more brain-friendly.

CHAPTER 5

Differentiated Instruction

The most important factor for differentiated instruction is recognition that even in a group of students with the same chronological age, each child is different. Today's students come to us with many differences: background knowledge, learning styles, interests, and skills, to name a few. One-size-fits-all learning is no longer seen as the way to reach students.

Tomlinson (1999) stated that differentiation can be accomplished in three areas: content (what the students need to learn), process (how they are going to learn), and product (how they are going to demonstrate that they have learned). It is an approach to teaching that requires the teacher to assess where the students are and start from that point by providing information and lessons in ways that solidly connect with the child's learning style and interests.

Fogarty (2001) suggests looking at differentiated instruction in three ways: change (content, process, product), challenge (emotions, attention, memory), and choice (freedom within structure). This is simply an elaboration of the basic concepts of differentiation with a focus on brain research.

Sprenger (2008) reminds us that we need to be aware of how the memory works to assist students at school and that learning styles and memory are closely linked.

Forsten, Grant, and Hollas (2002) state that there is no standard student profile, therefore no one specific way of teaching can meet the needs of all students. They explain five global strategies for differentiation: curriculum compacting, tiered activities, learning centers, flexible grouping, and mentoring.

A possible plan for use in differentiating instruction is tiered activities. Students are preassessed to see what they know. The teacher plans different kinds of instruction, structure, and support depending on the needs of the students. Ideally, tiered instruction should be challenging for all students. Group membership must be flexible, there should be several levels, and higher-order thinking skills should be utilized in every lesson.

29

Reis and Renzulli (2005) discuss that curriculum compacting is frequently associated with differentiated instruction. It is also used with gifted students. It means eliminating material that the student has already mastered and streamlining new lessons for the student to work at a comfortable pace based on ability and motivation. It is still important to follow curricular goals and offer appropriate options.

To meet the needs of all learners, meaningful exercises and lessons should be available all the time. In the early elementary grades, these opportunities are available in learning centers. In upper elementary and middle school, the activities and projects can be called smart stations, learning files, or project boxes, among others. Regardless of what they are called, they should contain meaningful, challenging opportunities for students to stretch their learning—individually or in pairs or small teams.

Forsten, Grant, and Hollas (2003) remind teachers that to differentiate effectively, it is necessary to look closely at textbooks. Teachers must take into consideration the learning styles of their students and provide appropriate strategies for success with content-heavy, boring, and difficult texts.

Hollas (2005) declares that differentiated instruction must rely on frequent assessments. Formative assessments are the key, and they must be ongoing. If the student takes the pretest and demonstrates that he already knows the material, then he should move on. If he is required to participate in the lessons and the "learning" again, he is not being respected as a learner. The results of the pretest on certain material for the entire class could provide the grouping structure for teaching and learning that material. The groups must be flexible because they could be different after pretesting the next skill. Tomlinson, in an interview with Rebora (2008), states that learners must be respected and teachers should be "teaching up" by giving their students challenging, stimulating, and thought-provoking material and then supporting those who need assistance.

Holland (2000) says that the way to a faster connection to material and success with learning is through the students' interests. It is important for the teacher to know the students well to understand their interests but also their learning styles. If they are visual learners then that is the best way to present the material as well as ask for the product.

Schweizer and Kossow (2007) share information about the usefulness of WebQuests as a differentiation tool. They provide the opportunity for authentic activities and the use of Internet-based information and resources to deepen understandings and stretch thinking about any topic imaginable.

Tomlinson and McTighe (2006) have joined together to present an interesting partnership—differentiated instruction and Understanding by Design. The two concepts work well together because both focus on where you want to be when the unit is completed. Differentiated instruction presents a clear way to get there. Both differentiated instruction and understanding by design depend on evidence of student learning, preassessment, learner differences, affective needs, flexibility in planning, and classroom routines.

Annotated Resources

Fogarty, Robin. *Differentiated Learning: Different Strokes for Different Folks.* Fogarty & Associates, 2001.
> Fogarty looks at differentiated learning in three ways: change (content, process, product), challenge (emotions, attention, memory), and choice (freedom within structure).

Forsten, Char, Jim Grant, & Betty Hollas. *Differentiated Instruction: Different Strategies for Different Learners, Grades K–8.* Crystal Springs Books, 2002.
> The book challenges the one-size-fits-all way of thinking. There is no standard student profile, and so no one specific way of teaching will meet the needs of all learners. All students are different, and therefore we need different strategies for different learners. These are the five global strategies

explained in the book: curriculum compacting, tiered activities, learning centers, flexible grouping, and mentoring.

Forsten, Char, Jim Grant, & Betty Hollas. *Differentiating Textbooks: Strategies to Improve Student Comprehension and Motivation.* Crystal Springs Books, 2003.
> This book gives helpful ways to address textbooks when dealing with students with different learning styles and needs. It suggests ways to create random groupings, to adapt textbooks, and before, during, and after reading strategies.

Gregory, Gayle, & Carolyn Chapman. *Differentiated Instructional Strategies: One Size Doesn't Fit All.* Corwin Press, 2002.
> This book provides information on planning for differentiated instruction, levels of thinking, and learning styles.

Hollas, Betty. *Differentiating Instruction in a Whole-Group Setting: Taking Easy First Steps into Differentiation.* Crystal Springs Books, 2005.
> There are four windows for differentiation: student engagement, questioning, flexible grouping, and ongoing assessment. This resource gives important information and practical activities for each.

Reis, Sally M., & Joseph S. Renzulli. *Curriculum Compacting: An Easy Start to Differentiating for High-Potential Students.* Prufrock Press, 2005.
> Everything you wanted to know about curriculum compacting, including the definition, how to use it, and how to implement it in the classroom.

Sprenger, Marilee. *Differentiation through Learning Styles and Memory.* Corwin Press, 2008.
> Sprenger talks about creating environments for learning, getting to know students' learning styles and how they remember, and differentiation for the visual/auditory and kinesthetic learner.

Tomlinson, Carol Ann. *The Differentiated Classroom: Responding to the Needs of All Learners.* Association for Supervision and Curriculum Development, 1999.
> This book explains how you can meet the diverse needs of all the students in your classroom. Tomlinson describes the five key concepts: content, process, product, affect, and learning environment. Implementing differentiated instruction empowers students to learn through multiple and varied opportunities for practice.

Tomlinson, Carol Ann. *How to Differentiate Instruction in Mixed-Ability Classrooms.* Association for Supervision and Curriculum Development, 2001.
> Tomlinson first clarifies what differentiated instruction is and isn't, then she discusses the rationale, role of the teacher, learning environment, strategies, how to plan interesting lessons, and how to differentiate content.

Tomlinson, Carol, & Jay McTighe. *Integrating Differentiated Instruction and Understanding by Design: Connecting Content and Kids.* Association for Supervision and Curriculum Development, 2006.
> The authors draw a parallel between the two concepts, showing that they are very similar and noting the importance of knowing where you want to be by the end of a certain unit or skill set.

Wormeli, Rick. *Differentiation: From Planning to Practice Grades 6–12.* Stenhouse Publishers, 2007.
> Wormeli begins with a frame of reference about differentiated instruction and includes a sample of a differentiated lesson; he next suggests helpful structures and strategies, he then

includes cognitive science structures and tips and finishes with twelve samples of differentiated learning experiences from multiple subjects.

Annotated Journal Articles

Carolan, Jennifer, and Abigail Guinn. "Differentiation: Lessons from Master Teachers." *Educational Leadership* (February 2007): 44–46.

Observing master teachers who are comfortable with differentiation is the best way for reluctant teachers to learn. It is important to offer personalized scaffolding, flexible means, good mentoring relationships, and subject-area expertise to develop a differentiated program.

Holland, Holly. "Reaching All Learners: You've Got to Know Them to Show Them." *Middle Ground* (April 2000): 1–3.

The author states that regardless of what you call it, the term "differentiated instruction" is not as important as the goal, which is helping students succeed by any means necessary. Students need choices, to be shown examples of quality work, and to be given opportunities to revise assignments; they need teachers who are always challenging them. In a differentiated instruction classroom, the teacher accepts all students where they are and then challenges them to be all they can be.

Moran, Seana, Mindy Kornhaber, & Howard Gardner. "Orchestrating Multiple Intelligences." *Educational Leadership* (September 2006): 23–27.

The nine multiple intelligences define the ways the mind works, no need to provide specific experiences in each. Just provide rich and collaborative experiences to all students and watch them go!

Rebora, Anthony. "Making a Difference." *Teacher Magazine* (September 10, 2008). Available at http://www.teachermagazine.org/tsb/articles/2008/09/10/01tomlinson.h02.html.

In this interview with differentiated instruction guru Carol Ann Tomlinson, she explains why we need differentiated instruction now. She highly recommends keeping kids in the classroom and attending to their readiness, their interests, and their preferred ways of learning. To be effective in the classroom, the teacher needs to really talk to the students and learn all about them. A teacher needs to be respectful of the students as learners.

Schweizer, Heidi, & Ben Kossow. "WebQuests: Tools for Differentiation." *Gifted Child Today* (Winter 2007): 29–35.

According to this article, to today's kids, digital technology is no more intimidating than a toaster. WebQuests were first created in 1995 by Bernie Dodge, and they are now more useful than ever for differentiation. They provide authentic activities that require the use of Internet-based resources to deepen understanding and stretch thinking about any topic imaginable.

Tomlinson, Carol Ann. "The Goals of Differentiation." *Educational Leadership* (November 2008): 26–30.

According to Tomlinson, we use differentiated instruction to ensure that all students master content. It is important that the teacher knows the learning destination of each student. The teacher must monitor each student's progress toward learning goals. Teachers must build trust, ensure fit, strengthen voice and develop awareness. Differentiated instruction helps develop student efficacy and ownership of learning.

Wormeli, Rick. "Busting Myths about Differentiated Instruction." *Principal Leadership* (March 2005): 28–29.

> Wormeli states that students who are taught using differentiated instruction will be prepared to take tests, that differentiated instruction does not mean changing the students' workload, that differentiation does not mean individualization, and that there are many ways to differentiate. It is important that students can show skill mastery at different times, and it is not what teachers teach that is important; the focus should be on what students learn. Formative, not summative, assessment is the key. For students to be successful learners, we need to differentiate.

CHAPTER 6

Differentiated Instruction in Reading

It seems that reading was always taught using reading groups based on the student's proficiency in oral reading and comprehension. Each class had three groups, and depending on the grade level, phonics was sometimes used as well as sight words. Then we seemed to become involved more in reading programs, some of which wanted the whole class to read the entire story together, stopping frequently to question, summarize, and then predict what would happen next before continuing the reading. At other times, we taught students to read using only phonics and decodable texts. We have since discovered that phonics is not a reading program but just one tool in a large toolbox of techniques for teaching reading.

With differentiated instruction in reading, one of the most important factors is student choice in selecting literature. The teacher and the media specialist are key in providing good books and the tools to finding and selecting a "just right" book. Skills can be pretested and then taught using literature as the lesson format rather than worksheets.

Currently we are hearing a great deal about guided reading instruction in which the teacher works with small flexible groups teaching reading strategies. Leveled books are the key component in a guided reading program. They are not selected from a collection of chapter books/novels and then leveled. Instead, they have been carefully written in accordance with standardized criteria for each level including difficulty level and words selected from an appropriate list (like controlled readers).

Miller (2008) cautions teachers regarding single-minded use of leveled books. She says it is helpful to know a student's comfort zone, and it is helpful to be able to direct students to appropriate books. However, students should not be labeled by their level. She feels it is better to provide a student with the tools to self-select an appropriate book and allow them to stop reading if the book is not a good match.

Reading experts such as Krashen (2004; annotated in Chapter 1), Allington (2001), Routman (2003; both annotated in Chapter 2), and others have confirmed that the only way to learn to read is using real literature and by helping children to select "just right" books. To provide the best possible climate for reinforcing beginning readers' improvement, it is necessary to focus on children's literature, classroom libraries, and teaching children to tell whether a book is just right for them. Students can and should select and read challenging books successfully especially if the topic is of great interest.

Most all of the steps and components for differentiated instruction in general can be applied to teaching reading using differentiated instruction. Robb (2008) reminds us that it is necessary to provide ongoing informal reading assessment to each student. Valuing independent reading for practice is important, as is meaningful teacher read-aloud selections. Organizing instruction is important so that students at all reading levels have appropriate instruction. Flexible small groups and pairs are an important part of differentiated reading instruction. Classroom management is important so that all students work effectively.

Carbo (2007) says that a great reading teacher uses differentiated strategies such as providing materials to stretch all students in reading with the highest-level and most appealing literature. She suggests that teachers form book clubs based on genres so that students can share their reading with classmates. She stresses literacy-rich environments in which attention to student learning styles and interests are emphasized.

Chapman and King (2003) focus on differentiation in teaching reading in the content areas and stress the importance of training these content-oriented teachers to be knowledgeable of ways they can help their students be more successful in reading-rich classes. Much the same principles are stressed: a positive climate for reading, knowing your students as readers, being able to model successful content area reading, and attention to both vocabulary study and comprehension assistance.

Tyner (2004) suggests that there are gaps in the guided reading model as we know it and proposes a small-group differentiated model that includes a variety of reading strategies, systematic word study, sight-word knowledge, and writing.

Brassell and Rasinski (2008; annotated in Chapter 1) share ideas about teaching comprehension successfully. They want to ensure that students have deep understanding of their reading, and they know the importance of engaging readers. In their book, they provide 50 terrific teacher tools and ideas for differentiation. The ideas are organized by topic: readiness, interest, learning profile, environment, content, activities (process), and product.

According to Walpole and McKenna (2007), it is important to understand the four types of assessments (screening, diagnostic, progress monitoring, and outcome). Each provides valuable information for differentiating instruction as reading is taught. With the results, we can look closely at each child's capabilities in the areas of phonemic awareness, word recognition, fluency, vocabulary, and comprehension. We can then match our instruction with those areas of specific needs.

What about media specialists? Media specialists work closely with teachers to provide exciting choices for students. They explore all the most recent titles and share them. They know the reading habits of students and help to guide them to the kind of books they select most often or to books by an author they like. They provide access to national programs for the entire student population. These include National Library Week, Teen Read Week, Read across America, Banned Books Week, Teen Tech Week, Reading across Continents, One Book–One School, and Read for the Record.

According to Hudak (2008), because the media specialist has a huge collection of learning resources, in many formats and at many learning levels, it stands to reason that they will be assisting students in understanding these resources and using them to full advantage to learn. Media specialists assist students in reading to find information for reports and projects. They help students to read to learn by showing them how to use a cataloging system and other databases and to find reliable search engines and Web sites. Once the students have found the materials they want to use, media specialists help them to search inside the books for tables of contents, indices, glossaries, and lists of references. They teach using Bloom's Taxonomy by helping students to understand, analyze, synthesize, and evaluate the material they find in their research. They help the students to find meaning in the information.

Annotated Resources

Carbo, Marie. *Becoming a Great Teacher of Reading: Achieving High Rapid Reading Gains with Powerful, Differentiated Strategies*. Corwin Press, 2007.

> Carbo begins with the focus point that all students can learn. She suggests teaching to students' natural strengths and using a continuum of reading methods. The Carbo Reading Method is described in detail. There is also information on active learning, visual dyslexia, and preparing students for tests.

Chapman, Carolyn, & Rita King. *Differentiated Instructional Strategies for Reading in the Content Areas*. Corwin Press, 2003.

> The key to successful differentiation in the content areas is attention to the climate, knowing the reader, various reading models, vocabulary, and word analysis.

Robb, Laura. *Differentiating Reading Instruction: How to Teach Reading to Meet the Needs of Each Student*. Scholastic, 2008.

> This resource covers reaching all learners with best practice teaching; the foundations for differentiated reading instruction; whole-class, small-group, and independent reading instruction; and writing instruction.

Tyner, Beverly. *Small-Group Reading Instruction: A Differentiated Reading Model for Beginning and Struggling Readers*. International Reading Association, 2004.

> This resource describes beginning reading instruction in small groups using the differentiated reading model, planning and assessing, instructional strategies, the different stages of reading (emergent, beginning, fledgling, transitional, and independent), early reading screening instruments, and word study.

Tyner, Beverly, & Sharon Green. *Small-Group Reading Instruction: A Differentiated Teaching Model for Intermediate Readers, Grades 3–8*. International Reading Association, 2005.

> This resource describes instruction in small groups using the differentiated reading model, the different stages of reading (evolving, maturing, advanced), assessment, and management.

Walpole, Sharon, & Michael McKenna. *Differentiated Reading Instruction: Strategies for the Primary Grades*. Guilford Press, 2007.

> This resource focuses on differentiating reading instruction for the primary grades by using assessments, differentiating phonemic awareness instruction, and building word recognition, fluency, vocabulary, and comprehension. It provides lesson plans for kindergarten through third grades.

Annotated Journal Articles

Armstrong, Thomas. "Making the Words Roar." *Educational Leadership* (March 2004): 78–81.

> This article gives reading strategies for each of the multiple intelligences.

Camilli, Gregory, & Paula Wolfe. "Research on Reading: A Cautionary Tale." *Educational Leadership* (March 2004): 26–29.

> This article points out that the National Reading Panel Report on Reading places far too much emphasis on systematic phonics. The author suggests that teachers should incorporate phonics into a broader plan of differentiated instruction. It is necessary first to assess students' needs and then their learning styles and to use a variety of approaches for success.

Christy, Janice. "Differentiating Reading Instruction in the Language Arts Classroom." *Teaching Today.* Available at http://www.glencoe.com/sec/teachingtoday/subject/diff_reading_la.phtml.

The author suggests starting the year by assessing each student's reading ability. She then provides suggestions for how to help all the readers in the class—struggling, general, and advanced.

Franklin, Pat, & Claire Stephens. "Get Students to Read through Booktalking." *School Library Media Activities Monthly* (March 2008): 38–39.

Start a booktalk program at your school to get kids interested in books. Take advantage of your school news program to booktalk great titles. The media specialist should set the tone by teaching students how to booktalk and then do a booktalk every time the students come to the media center. This article lists a number of tips for getting started with booktalking.

Hudak, Tina. "Are Librarians Reading Teachers, Too?" *Library Media Connection* (February 2008): 10–14.

Librarians are fundamentally reading teachers. They teach kids how to find information, find meaning, select what they need, and create reports and projects. Librarians are reading teachers for informational texts.

Ivey, Gay. "Redesigning Reading Instruction." *Educational Leadership* (September 2000): 42–45.

Ivey says that differentiating reading instruction can no longer be seen as an intervention; it is the way to teach and reach all students. All struggling readers need to get many opportunities to read and write—skill work alone will not make a difference. Ivey says that round-robin reading does little to help kids with fluency and skills. More resources should be used to expand the literature collection available to students, and schools should be looking for better reading teachers rather than better reading programs. A top priority should be given to time to read during the school day.

Koechlin, Carol, & Sandi Zwaan. "Everyone Wins: Differentiation in the School Library." *Teacher Librarian* (June 2008): 8–13.

The school librarian is a curriculum specialist who can provide a wide variety of materials to meet the needs of every learner. The library is filled with resources, flexible spaces, technology tools, and materials for many kinds of instructional strategies.

Miller, Donalyn. "Readers Seek Their Own Level." *Teacher Magazine* (November 4, 2008). Available at http://blogs.edweek.org/teachers/book_whisperer.

Miller discusses the dangers of the single-mindedness of teachers and leveling books. She says students should be given tools to make their own book selections and be allowed to select a book because of their interests.

Towle, Wendy. "The Art of Reading Workshop." *Educational Leadership* (September 2000): 38–41.

Towle states that reading workshop provides a framework for meeting the needs of all readers in the classroom. A reading workshop consists of time for teacher sharing, a focus lesson, state of the class conference, self-selected reading and responding time, and student sharing. Independent reading is the heart of reading workshop.

Wormeli, Rick. "Differentiating for Tweens." *Educational Leadership* (April 2006): 14–19.

Words of advice from the author: teach to developmental needs, treat academic struggle as strength, provide multiple pathways to standards, give formative feedback, and dare to be unconventional.

CHAPTER 7

Reading Tomorrow

The data about reading for pleasure is disturbing. Not enough teens, young adults, and adults read for pleasure. Everyone needs to be involved in making reading a pleasurable experience. Readers are good test takers and writers and have well-developed vocabularies. They do well in the workplace.

Parents should read aloud daily to and with their children and engage in story discussion after reading as soon as children talk. Frequent trips to the public library or bookstore are recommended. At both locations, children can participate in storytimes.

At school, reading should include lots of choices, frequent trips to the school library, a large, rotating classroom library, booklists of suggested titles and a reading log to record books read and reflections about the reading experience.

The whole school must get involved and that includes all faculty and administration. The school should have comfortable areas to read inside and outside. Time should be made to allow frequent all-school reading, guest readers, and book clubs of all sorts. If there is a school Web site, a TV studio, and a Parents' Association, all should reflect and support a commitment to reading enjoyment.

Atwell (2007), as reported in her book called *The Reading Zone,* has interviewed middle school students to understand their definitions of the "zone." The end result is teens who love to read, do it effortlessly, and model good reading habits for others. It includes time to read at school, the availability of trillions of great books, booktalks from peers, and a comfortable place to read.

Another important reading group is boys, and much has been written about them and their lack of interest in reading. Atwell in her book, Welch (2007) in his book, *The Guy-Friendly YA Library,* and Knowles and Smith (2005) in *Boys and Literacy* understand that boys have a special issue with reading and that greater efforts need to be made to encourage them to become avid pleasure readers.

Knowles and Smith (1997) share a whole-school reading plan aimed at bringing reading to the forefront, especially for middle school students among whom the disconnect can be great.

To increase the chances that middle-level students will read, it is necessary to put all the things shared in this book so far into a plan. The plan should be simple, straightforward, and easy to implement. It should have the full support of the administration and middle-level faculty. Over time, once all parts of the plan are in place, there should be an increase in the level of interest in reading for middle-level students.

- Read Aloud—at least once a week—with all members of the school community serving as readers

- Drop Everything and Read (DEAR)—fifteen minutes a day, every day, perhaps alternating classes, subject areas, or time periods, and all students should have a personal selection reading time as part of homework

- Media Center Reading Environment—special area, special seating, display titles, advisory board of middle-level students to help make ordering selections, review books, display new titles, include magazine rack with student-selected magazines, display of student-created books

- Classroom Reading Environment—reading area with special seating, books available, attention to a wide variety of titles incorporated within all content areas, time to read, time to talk about books

- School Community—all-school reading time, benches available for reading outside

- Web page—page for Media Center where students post reviews and the media specialist can introduce new titles, promotions, general information, and lists of links of interest to young adults

- TV Production Studio—shows, panel discussions on books, information on authors, reading trivia games/contests

- Publishing Center—where writers can produce books for peers and younger students

- Book Clubs—for teachers to read and discuss YA literature, for students to get together to all read one title or one author or on one subject and then share ideas and thoughts on their readings, for parents, students, grade levels, etc.

- Curriculum Changes—to include literature in all content areas, encouraging all content area teachers to teach reading strategies, to allow students time to read

- More Curriculum Changes—to help traditional English literature teachers include YA fiction to compare and contrast with classics, to emphasize students responding to literature on a personal level through literature circles and response journals, to explore reading workshops where students select their own reading material and work at their own pace and where skill teaching is done on an as-needed basis

- Visual Literacy—students should be taught to gather information and construct their own charts, graphs and diagrams, they need instruction in organizing large amounts of information—with special training in the use of a wide variety of graphic organizers, students also need to be taught skimming, scanning, note taking, and summarizing

- Information Literacy—a research process such as Big 6 should be taught and tied to the curriculum; library media specialists, computer teachers, and classroom teachers must work together to develop units and lessons that will include computer skills, information skills, and content-area curriculum outcomes

- Special Events—connecting music and literature with plays, meaningful field trips, older students reading to and writing for younger students and vice versa, author and illustrator visits

- Booktalks—librarians, teachers, and students all sharing a brief and tantalizing glimpse of excellent titles to promote reading

- Professional Development—sending teachers to reading conferences and workshops, creating opportunities to visit schools and libraries with good teen reading programs, encouraging memberships in professional reading organizations, building professional libraries with lots of good books on reading, and obtaining professional journals for reading and discussion at faculty meetings

- State-Sponsored Reading Programs—Florida has Sunshine State Readers—where students read from a short list and vote on their favorite titles

- Bookshare—circulation of used books: kids bring in old books and buy back others for 50 cents each; teachers can have copies for classroom libraries, and the leftovers can be donated to local charities

- Free Shelves—used books for students and teachers to take and replace with one of their own

- Audio Books, Magazines, and Graphic Novels—should be part of a library collection for young adults

Preparing our children to be lifelong readers is everyone's responsibility. Many organizations are dedicated to putting books in the hands of all children and their families. Here are a few:

Kids Reading to Kids—a National Program for Character Development and Reading Improvement: http://www.kidsreadingtokids.org

- The organization's membership includes more than 1,200 schools in the United States and throughout the world (program started September 2006).

- It focuses on the development of underachievers and making every kid a role model.

- Its Web site contains information for teachers and parents.

Reach Out and Read National Center—"Children are better prepared for school if their parents read to them engagingly": http://www.reachoutandread.org

- Reach Out and Read programs frequently use donated books.

- Its focus is on children between the ages of 6 months and 5 years.

- More than 50,000 doctors have given 20 million free books to America's youngest children living in poverty through the Reach Out and Read Program.

- It was founded in 1989 by doctors.

Jumpstart—"Working toward the day every child in America enters school prepared to succeed": http://www.jstart.org

- Read for the Record (www.readfortherecord.org)—one day, one book, for children everywhere.

- Jumpstart trains adults to read with children and include conversation about the reading.

- Asking children open-ended questions is the key.

- The Web site includes reading tips tools for families and activities,

Reading Is Fundamental—Creating literacy-rich homes for all children: http://www.rif.org

- Founded in 1966, RIF is the oldest and largest children's and family nonprofit literacy organization in the United States.

- RIF's highest priority is reaching underserved children from birth to age 8.

- Through community volunteers in every state and U.S. territory, RIF provides 4.5 million children with 16 million new, free books and literacy resources each year.

- Its Web site provides printable parent guides and information about motivating kids to read, school connections, activities, and further Web resources.

The National Center for Family Literacy—Creating a literate nation by leveraging the power of the family: http://www.famlit.org

- NCFL pioneered the approach that puts family at the forefront of educational reform.

- Since its inception in 1989, NCFL has provided the leadership to solve our national literacy problem.

- Through groundbreaking initiatives, NCFL fuels life improvement for the nation's most disadvantaged children and parents.

- More than 1 million families throughout the country have made positive educational and economic gains as a result of NCFL's work, which includes training more than 150,000 teachers and thousands of volunteers.

National Head Start Association: http://www.nhsa.org/

- The National Head Start Association is a private not-for-profit membership organization dedicated exclusively to meeting the needs of Head Start children and their families.

- It represents more than 1 million children, 200,000 staff and 2,700 Head Start programs in the United States.

- Created in 1965, Head Start is the most successful, longest-running, national school readiness program in the United States.

- It provides comprehensive education, health, nutrition, and parent involvement services to low-income children and their families.

- Nearly 25 million preschool-age children have benefited from Head Start.

http://www.rosemarywells.com/

This popular young children's author, Rosemary Wells, has some very cute advice for parents on her Web page. Her "Read to Your Bunny" pages include a wonderful essay called, "The Most Important Twenty Minutes of Your Day," one titled simply, "Children at Risk," and a very informative piece called,

"What the Experts Say." All of these can be copied and handed out to parents and teachers and should be because they contain very useful information.

Annotated Resources

Atwell, Nancie. *The Reading Zone: How to Help Kids Become Skilled, Passionate, Habitual, Critical Readers.* Scholastic, 2007.

    Atwell, an author with a focus on middle school students, tells how to get students of this age to enjoy reading and to read successfully. Topics include in the zone, choice, comprehension, booktalking, boys and reading, and high school.

Chapman, Anne. *Making Sense: Critical Reading across the Curriculum.* The College Board, 1993.

    This book defines ten areas—here are eight: foster reading with understanding, encourage wide reading, use multicultural stories, talk to readers about their reading, observe how kids read, avoid nagging and criticizing, mistakes are OK, and help students make positive changes in their reading habits.

Knowles, Elizabeth, & Martha Smith. *Boys and Literacy: Practical Strategies for Librarians, Teachers, and Parents.* Libraries Unlimited, 2005.

    Eleven topics are explored specifically for boys, and the text includes discussion questions, an annotated and a regular bibliography, and also author information and a list of magazines for boys.

Knowles, Elizabeth, & Martha Smith. *Reading Rules! Motivating Teens to Read.* Libraries Unlimited, 2001.

    Filled with ideas, practical tips, useful statistics, and other helpful data on teen reading, this book details numerous methods for getting teens to read, such as reading workshops, literature circles, book clubs, and booktalks. An overview of YA literature and annotated bibliographies of both teen and professional reads further assists in creating a literacy plan.

Welch, Rollie James. *The Guy-Friendly YA Library: Serving Male Teens.* Libraries Unlimited, 2007.

    This is a wonderful resource for librarians and teachers of male teens. The topics include understanding teen males, their reading habits, books they like, providing library programs for them, booktalks, and a great list of popular titles for teen males.

Annotated Journal Articles

Arnold, Renea, & Nell Colburn. "First Steps: The Perfect Partner—Head Start Is an Ideal Ally for Promoting Early Literacy." *School Library Journal* (March 2007). Available at http://www.schoollibraryjournal.com/article/CA6420399.html.

    It is important for libraries to provide services for children beginning with the very early years. Therefore, a partnership with the Head Start program is vital to getting the word out about the importance of reading aloud to children.

Feldman, Sari, & Dr. Robert Needlman. "Take Two Board Books and Call Me in the Morning." *School Library Journal* (June 1999): 30–33.

    Pediatricians are now telling new parents to read to their children early and very often. They are supporting programs to provide books for all children.

Gambrell. Linda. "Patterson, Proust, and the Power of Pleasure Reading." *Reading Today* (February 2008): 18.

    Gambrell enjoys reading the Sunday newspaper and found an article by best-selling author James Patterson, who says it is the responsibility of all parents, grandparents and teachers to introduce children to books that they will not be able to put down. She also read about Marcel Proust who believed that reading is a sanctuary. Two of the most disturbing statistics are how few Americans read for pleasure and that we are spending less and less time reading. As a result, comprehension skills are declining, and Gambrell thinks we should be very concerned.

Gambrell, Linda. "Promoting Pleasure Reading: The Role of Models, Mentors, and Motivators." *Reading Today* (August 2007): 16.

    Gambrell, the president of the International Reading Association, states that teachers should demonstrate a love of reading, they should use a broad range of techniques to mentor students into the reading community, and should encourage students to read a lot.

Hart, Betty, & Todd Risley. "The Early Catastrophe: The 30 Million Word Gap by Age Three." *American Educator* (Spring 2003). Available at http://www.aft.org/american_educator/spring2003/catastrophe.html.

    This article gives statistics that are old but still meaningful. Underprivileged children by the age of three years are seriously behind in talk, vocabulary growth, and interaction with the written word. Starting out this way requires serious intervention to get these children reading during the first few years of school.

Neuman, Susan B. "N Is for Nonsensical." *Educational Leadership* (October 2006): 28–31.

    Low-income preschool children need content-rich instruction. It is critical to close the knowledge gap with time, materials, and resources. Opportunities for in-depth learning, high levels of teacher interaction, and a supportive learning environment are all absolutely necessary to close the gap.

Lesson Plans PK–3

Title: *A Dictionary of Dance*
Author: Liz Murphy
Publisher: Blue Apple Books
Date: 2007
ISBN #: 1593546130
Genre: Nonfiction
Synopsis: Everything about dance organized alphabetically with wonderful illustrations.
Audience: Grades K–3
Curricular Connections
Topics: Dance, Dictionary
Discussion Questions and Journal Prompts:
What did you learn about dance from this book?
What is your favorite dance word and why?
Which picture did you like best and why?
Activities for Differentiated Instruction:
Create a poster about the book.
Draw a picture from the book and write one sentence to describe it.
Write a letter to the author telling what you liked about the book.

Title: *A Father Like That*
Author: Charlotte Zolotow
Author Web Site: http://www.charlottezolotow.com
Publisher: HarperCollins
Date: 2007
ISBN #: 0060278641
Genre: Fiction
Synopsis: A young boy shares with his mother his daydreams about the father who left before he was born.
Audience: Grades K–2
Curricular Connections
Topics: Fathers and Sons, Single-Parent Families
Discussion Questions and Journal Prompts:
Did you agree or disagree with the boy?
Did you enjoy the story? Why or why not?
If you were the author, how would you change the story?
Activities for Differentiated Instruction:
Write a letter to the boy in the book.
Create a drawing that shows a "daydream" from the book.
Make a list of ten describing words (adjectives) from the book.

From *Differentiating Reading Instructing Using Children's Literature* by Liz Knowles, Ed.D. Santa Barbara, CA: Libraries Unlimited. Copyright © 2009.

Title: *Alvin Ho: Allergic to Girls, School and Other Scary Things*
Author: Lenore Look
Publisher: Random/Schwartz
Date: 2008
ISBN #: 0375839143
Genre: Fiction
Synopsis: A young boy in Concord, Massachusetts, who loves superheroes and comes from a long line of brave Chinese farmer-warriors, wants to make friends, but first he must first overcome his fear of everything.
Audience: Grades 2–4
Curricular Connections
Topics: Chinese-American, Friendship, Self-confidence
Discussion Questions and Journal Prompts:
What did you like about this book? Explain.
What are you afraid of?
Which superheroes are your favorites?
Activities for Differentiated Instruction:
Create a poster about your favorite superhero.
Write a letter to the main character giving him some advice.
Make an acrostic with words from the book.

Title: *Angelina's Island*
Author: Jeanette Winter
Publisher: Farrar, Straus & Giroux/Frances Foster Books
Date: 2007
ISBN #: 0374303495
Genre: Fiction
Synopsis: Every day, Angelina dreams of her home in Jamaica and imagines she is there, until her mother finds a wonderful way to convince her that New York is now their home.
Audience: Grades K–2
Curricular Connections
Topics: Homesick, Jamaica, New York, Parades
Discussion Questions and Journal Prompts:
What did you learn from this book?
Have you ever been homesick? Describe your feelings.
Describe the main character.
Activities for Differentiated Instruction:
Create a travel brochure about Jamaica.
Create a parade with some of your classmates to tell about the book.
Write an illustrated poem about the book.

Title: *Bandit*
Author: Karen Rostoker-Gruber
Author Web Site: http://www.karenrostoker-gruber.com
Publisher: Marshall Cavendish
Date: 2008
ISBN #: 0761453822
Genre: Fiction
Synopsis: When Bandit's family moves to a new house, the cat runs away and returns to the only home he knows, but after he is brought back, he understands that the new house is now home.
Audience: Grades K–2
Curricular Connections
Topics: Cats, Moving
Discussion Questions and Journal Prompts:
What do you know about cats?
Is Bandit a good name for this cat? Why or why not?
Did you predict the ending?
Activities for Differentiated Instruction:
Make a list of adjectives (describing words) about cats.
Draw a suitcase for a cat and what would go inside. Label each thing a cat would take.
Find and read another story about a cat. How are they the same? Different?

Title: *Buffalo Music*
Author: Tracey E. Fern
Author Web Site: http://www.traceyfern.com/
Publisher: Clarion
Date: 2008
ISBN #: 0618723412
Genre: Fiction
Synopsis: After hunters kill off the buffalo around her Texas ranch, a woman begins raising orphan buffalo calves and eventually ships four members of her small herd to Yellowstone National Park, where they form the beginnings of newly thriving buffalo herds. Based on the true story of Mary Ann Goodnight and her husband Charles; includes author's note about her work, Web sites, and a bibliography.
Audience: Grades K–4
Curricular Connections
Topics: American Bison, Mary Ann Goodnight, Texas
Discussion Questions and Journal Prompts:
Why was it important to raise the orphan buffalo?
What did you learn from this story?
From reading this story, what do you know about Mary Ann Goodnight?
Activities for Differentiated Instruction:
Research Mary Ann Goodnight and tell your classmates about her.
Draw a poster for Yellowstone National Park. Do not forget to include some buffalo.
Make an acrostic for the word buffalo.

From *Differentiating Reading Instructing Using Children's Literature* by Liz Knowles, Ed.D.
Santa Barbara, CA: Libraries Unlimited. Copyright © 2009.

Title: *Elizabeth Leads the Way: Elizabeth Cady Stanton and the Right to Vote*
Author: Tanya Lee Stone
Author Web Site: http://www.tanyastone.com
Publisher: Henry Holt and Company
Date: 2008
ISBN #: 0805079033
Genre: Biography
Synopsis: Elizabeth, from an early age, knew that women were not given the same rights as men. So she went to college and became friends with a group of women who worked together to get women the right to vote.
Audience: Grades 1–4
Curricular Connections
Topics: Right to Vote for Women, Suffragists
Discussion Questions and Journal Prompts:
Why is this story important in American History?
What kind of person was Elizabeth Cady Stanton?
Why is it important for all registered voters to vote in elections?
Activities for Differentiated Instruction:
Create a timeline for Elizabeth Cady Stanton's life.
Draw a banner encouraging everyone to vote.
Write a poem about voting.

Title: *Frida: Viva la Vida! Long Live Life!*
Author: Carmen T. Bernier-Grand
Author Web Site: http://www.hevanet.com/grand/
Publisher: Marshall Cavendish
Date: 2007
ISBN #: 0761453369
Genre: Biographical Poems
Synopsis: Biographical poems about the famous Mexican artist, Frida Kahlo.
Audience: Grades PK–3
Award: Pura Belpre Author Honor Book 2008
Curricular Connections
Topics: Artist, Biography, Mexico, Poetry
Discussion Questions and Journal Prompts:
What did you learn about Frida Kahlo?
What do you like about Mexican art?
Do you like a story written in poetry? Why or why not?
Activities for Differentiated Instruction:
Draw a picture from the book.
Write your own poem about Frida Kahlo and her artwork.
Find Mexico on a map.

Title: *Hello, Bumblebee Bat*
Author: Darrin Lunde
Author Web Site: http://www.charlesbridge.com/client/client_pdfs/homepage/DarrinLundeQA.pdf
Publisher: Charlesbridge
Date: 2007
ISBN #: 1570913749
Genre: Nonfiction
Synopsis: Simple text and illustrations introduce the endangered bumblebee bat of Thailand.
Audience: Grades PK–3
Award: Theodor Seuss Geisel Award Honor Book 2008
Curricular Connections
Topics: Bats, Endangered Species
Discussion Questions and Journal Prompts:
What did you learn from this book?
Why is this particular bat endangered?
Is it important that we protect these bats? Why or why not?
Activities for Differentiated Instruction:
Do some research and then make a chart about the different kinds of bats.
Retell this story in pictures.
What a poem about the bumblebee bat.

Title: *Henry's Freedom Box*
Author: Ellen Levine
Author Web Site: http://www.scholastic.com/ellenlevine
Publisher: Scholastic
Date: 2007
ISBN #: 043977733X
Genre: Historical Fiction
Synopsis: A fictionalized account of how in 1849 a Virginia slave, Henry "Box" Brown, escapes to freedom by shipping himself in a wooden crate from Richmond to Philadelphia.
Audience: Grades PK–3
Award: Caldecott Medal Winner 2008
Curricular Connections:
Topics: 1800s, Multicultural, Racism and Prejudice
Discussion Questions and Journal Prompts:
Why did the author write this book?
What kind of person was Henry Brown?
Were there any surprises for you in this book?
Activities for Differentiated Instruction:
Read a part of this story to your class.
Create a story pyramid for the book (title, characters, setting, events, and ending).
Mark the distance from Richmond, Virginia, to Philadelphia, Pennsylvania, on a United States map.

From *Differentiating Reading Instructing Using Children's Literature* by Liz Knowles, Ed.D.
Santa Barbara, CA: Libraries Unlimited. Copyright © 2009.

Title: *Heroes for Civil Rights*
Author: David A. Adler
Author Web Site: http://www.davidaadler.com
Publisher: Holiday House
Date: 2008
ISBN #: 0823420086
Genre: Biography
Synopsis: This book gives biographical information on many people in history who championed the Civil Rights Movement.
Audience: Grades 3–5
Curricular Connections
Topics: African Americans, Civil Rights Workers
Discussion Questions and Journal Prompts:
Share three things that you learned from this book.
Name some characteristics shared by most of these heroes.
Why is this book important?
Activities for Differentiated Instruction:
Make a poster telling about one of these people.
Create a timeline for the Civil Rights Movement.
Create a ten-word crossword puzzle about the book.

Title: *Hurry! Hurry!*
Author: Eve Bunting
Author Web Site: http://www.readingrockets.org/books/interviews/bunting
Publisher: Harcourt
Date: 2007
ISBN #: 0152054103
Genre: Fiction
Synopsis: All the animals of the barnyard community hurry to greet their newest member, who is just pecking his way out of an egg.
Audience: Grades K–1
Curricular Connections
Topics: Chickens, Eggs
Discussion Questions and Journal Prompts:
What other kinds of animals hatch from eggs?
What did you learn from this story?
Did you ever see an egg hatch? If so, describe it.
Activities for Differentiated Instruction:
Make a drawing from the story and label it.
Tell the story to your classmates.
Make an acrostic from the word "chicken."

Title: *Imaginary Menagerie: A Book of Curious Creatures*
Author: Julie Larios
Publisher: Harcourt
Date: 2008
ISBN #: 0152063250
Genre: Poetry
Synopsis: Poems about mythical creatures such as dragons, mermaids, trolls, thunderbirds, and the phoenix.
Audience: Grades 2–5
Curricular Connections
Topics: Children's Poetry, Mythical Creatures
Discussion Questions and Journal Prompts:
Which of these mythical creatures were new to you?
Did you like these poems? Why or why not?
Did the illustrations add to the book? Explain.
Activities for Differentiated Instruction:
Create your own poem about one of these mythical creatures.
Create an acrostic about the story.
Draw your own mythical creature and write a description of it.

Title: *Ivy and Bean Break the Fossil Record*
Author: Annie Barrows
Author Web Site: http://www.anniebarrows.com
Publisher: Chronicle Books
Date: 2007
ISBN #: 0811856836
Genre: Fiction
Synopsis: Everyone in second grade seems set on breaking a world record, and friends Ivy and Bean are no exception, deciding to become the youngest people ever to discover a dinosaur skeleton.
Audience: Grades 1–3
Curricular Connections
Topics: Fossils, Friendship, World Records
Discussion Questions and Journal Prompts:
What part did friendship play in this story?
Why do people always want to break world records?
What do you know about dinosaurs?
Activities for Differentiated Instruction:
Create an illustrated poem about a dinosaur.
Create a trophy for Ivy and Bean and their world record.
Write a letter to a friend recommending this book.

From *Differentiating Reading Instructing Using Children's Literature* by Liz Knowles, Ed.D.
Santa Barbara, CA: Libraries Unlimited. Copyright © 2009.

Title: *Jazz Baby*
Author: Lisa Wheeler
Author Web Site: http://www.lisawheelerbooks.com
Publisher: Harcourt
Date: 2007
ISBN #: 0152025227
Genre: Fiction
Synopsis: Baby and his family make some jazzy music.
Audience: Grades PK–3
Award: Theodor Seuss Geisel Award Honor Book 2008
Curricular Connections
Topics: Music, Rhymes
Discussion Questions and Journal Prompts:
How do the words and verses in the book make you feel?
What is the author saying in this book?
What is your favorite kind of music?
Activities for Differentiated Instruction:
Make a list of all the words in the book that show movement and sound.
Look at the author's Web site and tell your classmates about her.
Make a bookmark for this book.

Title: *Jazz on a Saturday Night*
Author: Leo and Diane Dillon
Author Web Site: http://www.kidsreads.com/authors/au-dillon-leo-diane.asp
Publisher: The Blue Sky Press
Date: 2007
ISBN #: 0590478931
Genre: Picture Book—Biography
Synopsis: Short informative pieces about all the great jazz musicians colorfully illustrated.
Audience: Grades PK–3
Award: Coretta Scott King Illustrator Award Honor Book 2008
Curricular Connections:
Topics: Music and Arts, Jazz Musicians
Discussion Questions and Journal Prompts:
What do you like about the illustrations? Do they add to the book?
Have you ever heard jazz music? Can you describe it?
What kinds of instruments do jazz musicians play?
Activities for Differentiated Instruction:
Write a poem about jazz.
Create a poster for this book.
Select one of the jazz musicians from the book and find out more.

Title: *Just Me and 6,000 Rats: A Tale of Conjunctions*
Author: Rick Walton
Author Web Site: http://www.rickwalton.com
Publisher: Gibbs Smith
Date: 2007
ISBN #: 1423602196
Genre: Fiction
Synopsis: A boy is surprised by people's reactions when he and six thousand rats visit a big city, in a tale that features conjunctions from "and" to "yet."
Audience: Grades K–2
Curricular Connections
Topics: Cities, Conjunctions, Rats, Towns
Discussion Questions and Journal Prompts:
Did this story help you to understand conjunctions?
Did you like the illustrations? Why or why not?
What other animal would you like to see in this story instead of rats? Why?
Activities for Differentiated Instruction:
Make an A-B-C book of the conjunctions in this story.
Draw a picture of the boy with 6,000 (or almost) of the other animal you selected.
Tell a friend about this book.

Title: *Kami and The Yaks*
Author: Andrea Stenn Stryer
Author Web Site: http://www.stryer.com
Publisher: Bay Otter Press
Date: 2007
ISBN #: 0977896102
Genre: Fiction
Synopsis: Kami, who is deaf, leaves his Sherpa family to search for their missing yaks. He tries whistling for them and then searches their favorite places. Just as a severe thunderstorm approaches Kami finds the missing yaks to the delight of his family.
Audience: Grades PK–3
Award: Schneider Family Book Award—Birth through Grade School 2008
Curricular Connections
Topics: Deafness, Himalayas, Sherpa
Discussion Questions and Journal Prompts:
How do deaf people manage in our noisy world?
Was Kami brave? Explain.
What things do you do to make your family happy?
Activities for Differentiated Instruction:
Find out about yaks. What do they do? Share with your classmates.
Where are the Himalaya Mountains? Draw a map to show where they are located.
Draw a picture from the story and write a sentence to describe it.

From *Differentiating Reading Instructing Using Children's Literature* by Liz Knowles, Ed.D.
Santa Barbara, CA: Libraries Unlimited. Copyright © 2009.

Title: *Knuffle Bunny Too: A Case of Mistaken Identity*
Author: Mo Willems
Author Web Site: http://www.mowillems.com/
Publisher: Hyperion Books for Children
Date: 2007
ISBN #: 1423102991
Genre: Fiction
Synopsis: Her daddy in tow, Trixie hurries to school to show off her one-of-a-kind Knuffle Bunny. But an awful surprise awaits her: someone else has the exact same bunny!
Audience: Grades K–1
Award: Caldecott Medal Honor Book 2008
Curricular Connections
Topics: Friendship, Sports, Stuffed Animals
Discussion Questions and Journal Prompts:
What have you brought to school to share?
Do you have a favorite stuffed animal? Tell about it.
What is your favorite part of the day at school?
Activities for Differentiated Instruction:
Bring in your favorite stuffed animal and tell the class about it.
Draw a picture of Knuffle Bunny and write the name.
Tell your classmates what you liked about this story.

Title: *Lazily, Crazily, Just a Bit Nasally: More about Adverbs*
Author: Brian P. Cleary
Author Web Site: http://www.brianpcleary.com
Publisher: Millbrook Press
Date: 2008
ISBN #: 0822578484
Genre: Nonfiction
Synopsis: Rhyming words and illustrations exemplify adverbs and their functions.
Audience: Grades 1–4
Curricular Connections
Topics: Adverbs, English Language
Discussion Questions and Journal Prompts:
Was the author successful? Do you understand about adverbs?
What did you think of the illustrations? Did they add to the book?
Can you now give the definition of an adverb? What is it?
Activities for Differentiated Instruction:
Create an A-B-C book about adverbs.
Make a poster about the author and his books.
Make an adverb acrostic.

Title: *Lightship*
Author: Brian Floca
Author Web Site: http://www.brianfloca.com
Publisher: Atheneum/Richard Jackson Books
Date: 2007
ISBN #: 1416924361
Genre: Nonfiction
Synopsis: Lightships once served where lighthouses could not be built. They helped to guide sailors safely through the fog.
Audience: Grades K–2
Award: Robert F. Silbert Honor Book 2008
Curricular Connections
Topics: Boats and Ships, Science and Nature, Transportation, Water
Discussion Questions and Journal Prompts:
Have you ever seen a lighthouse? What do they do?
What did you learn about sailors from this book?
What are some other things that fog does?
Activities for Differentiated Instruction:
Draw a picture of the story and tell about it.
Find another book about lighthouses and read it.
Make a chart of every kind of transportation you can think of.

Title: *Mercy Watson: Princess in Disguise*
Author: Kate DiCamillo
Author Web Site: http://www.katedicamillo.com
Publisher: Candlewick Press
Date: 2007
ISBN #: 0763630144
Genre: Fiction
Synopsis: Persuaded by the word "treating" to dress up as a princess for Halloween, Mercy the pig's trick-or-treat outing has some very unexpected results.
Audience: Grades K–2
Curricular Connections
Topics: Halloween, Humor, Pigs
Discussion Questions and Journal Prompts:
What happened to Mercy on Halloween?
What adventures have you had on Halloween?
What costumes/disguises have you had for Halloween?
Activities for Differentiated Instruction:
Draw a picture from the story and tell about it.
Dress up in a Halloween costume and tell this story to your class.
Make a Halloween acrostic.

From *Differentiating Reading Instructing Using Children's Literature* by Liz Knowles, Ed.D.
Santa Barbara, CA: Libraries Unlimited. Copyright © 2009.

Title: *Mr. Putter and Tabby Run the Race*
Author: Cynthia Rylant
Author Web Site: http://childrensbooks.about.com/cs/authorsillustrato/a/cynthiarylant.htm
Publisher: Harcourt
Date: 2008
ISBN #: 0152060693
Genre: Picture Book—Fiction
Synopsis: Mr. Putter is convinced to run in a senior marathon with his neighbor, Mrs. Teaberry, when he learns that second prize is a train set.
Audience: Grades 1–2
Curricular Connections
Topics: Cats, Neighbors, Old Age, Physical Fitness
Discussion Questions and Journal Prompts:
What did you like about this story?
What is a marathon?
Tell about Tabby's part in the story.
Activities for Differentiated Instruction:
Draw a picture of a train. Tell the class about the train in the story.
Make a poem about this story.
Make up a different ending to the story.

Title: *Mr. Putter and Tabby See the Stars*
Author: Cynthia Rylant
Author Web Site: http://childrensbooks.about.com/cs/authorsillustrato/a/cynthiarylant.htm
Publisher: Harcourt
Date: 2007
ISBN #: 0152063558
Genre: Fiction—Picture Books
Synopsis: When Mr. Putter cannot sleep after eating too many of Mrs. Teaberry's pineapple jelly rolls, he and Tabby take a moonlit stroll that ends with the perfect neighborly gathering.
Audience: Grades 1–3
Curricular Connections
Topics: Cats, Neighbors, Night
Discussion Questions and Journal Prompts:
What did you learn about Mr. Putter's neighbors from this story?
What is your favorite sweet to eat?
What kind of a friend is Tabby?
Activities for Differentiated Instruction:
Write your own story about a moonlight stroll.
Create a book mark to advertise the story.
Dress up as a story character and tell the story to your classmates.

Title: *My Colors, My World*
Author: Maya Christina Gonzalez
Author Web Site: http://www.mayagonzalez.com
Publisher: Children's Book Press
Date: 2007
ISBN #: 0892392215
Genre: Fiction
Synopsis: Maya, who lives in the dusty desert, opens her eyes wide to find the colors in her world, from Papi's black hair and Mami's orange and purple flowers to Maya's red swing set and the fiery pink sunset.
Audience: Grades PK–3
Award: Pura Belpre Illustrator Award Book 2008
Curricular Connections
Topics: Colors, Deserts, Spanish-Americans
Discussion Questions and Journal Prompts:
What was the best thing about this story?
What is your favorite color? Why?
Tell what you know about deserts.
Activities for Differentiated Instruction:
Make a booklet of colors you see in your world and where you see them.
Draw a picture from this book and write a sentence describing the picture.
Draw a rainbow.

Title: *Ocean Seasons*
Author: Ron Hirschi
Author Web Site: http://www.ronhirschi.com
Publisher: Sylvan Dell Publishers
Date: 2007
ISBN #: 0977742324
Genre: Nonfiction
Synopsis: Includes "For Creative Minds" section with food web cards and information on how seasonal changes affect ocean plants and animals.
Audience: Grades K–4
Curricular Connections
Topics: Food Chains, Marine Ecology
Discussion Questions and Journal Prompts:
Have you ever been to the ocean? What did you see?
What did you learn from this book?
What kinds of food come from the ocean? Give examples.
Activities for Differentiated Instruction:
Find out about the author from his Web site and create a poster about him and his books.
Make an A-B-C book with information about oceans.
Make a five-word crossword puzzle with words from the book.

From *Differentiating Reading Instructing Using Children's Literature* by Liz Knowles, Ed.D.
Santa Barbara, CA: Libraries Unlimited. Copyright © 2009.

Title: *Oh Theodore!: Guinea Pig Poems*
Author: Susan Katz
Author Web Site: http://www.netaxs.com/~Katz/
Publisher: Clarion Books
Date: 2007
ISBN #: 0618702220
Genre: Fiction—Poetry
Synopsis: Since his mother will not allow him to get a dog, a young boy has to settle for a guinea pig. Through short and easy-to-read poems, the reader will learn all about guinea pigs.
Audience: Grades K–3
Curricular Connections
Topics: Guinea Pigs, Poems
Discussion Questions and Journal Prompts:
What did you learn about guinea pigs?
Tell about the boy in the story. What kind of a pet owner was he?
Tell about your pet.
Activities for Differentiated Instruction:
Write a poem about your pet.
Make an acrostic about guinea pigs.
Draw a poster about this book so that others will want to read it.

Title: *Quirky, Jerky, Extra Perky: More about Adjectives*
Author: Brian P. Cleary
Author Web Site: http://www.brianpcleary.com
Publisher: Millbrook Press
Date: 2007
ISBN #: 0822567097
Genre: Nonfiction
Synopsis: An introduction to adjectives and how they help with descriptions.
Audience: Grades 2–4
Curricular Connections
Topics: Adjectives, English Language
Discussion Questions and Journal Prompts:
What did you learn from this book?
How did the illustrations work in the book?
Tell about the author and his other books.
Activities for Differentiated Instruction:
Make an A-B-C book of adjectives.
Create an acrostic using adjectives.
Write a letter to the author telling what you liked about the book.

Title: *Skunkdog*
Author: Emily Jenkins
Author Web Site: http://www.emilyjenkins.com
Publisher: Farrar, Straus & Giroux
Date: 2008
ISBN #: 0374370095
Genre: Fiction
Synopsis: Dumpling, a lonely dog with no sense of smell, moves with his family to the country and makes a new friend who takes some getting used to.
Audience: Grades K–3
Curricular Connections
Topics: Dogs, Friendship, Skunks
Discussion Questions and Journal Prompts:
How is friendship important in this story?
What did you learn about skunks in this story?
What was the best part of this story?
Activities for Differentiated Instruction:
Write a different ending for this story.
Write an illustrated poem about Dumpling.
Design a poster advertisement for this story.

Title: *So Said Ben*
Author: Michael McCurdy
Author Web Site: http://www.michaelmccurdy.com
Publisher: Creative Editions
Date: 2008
ISBN #: 156846147X
Genre: Biography
Synopsis: Profiles Benjamin Franklin, who was an inventor, scientist, printer, and statesman.
Audience: Grades 1–6
Curricular Connections
Topics: Inventors, Ben Franklin, Scientists, Statesmen
Discussion Questions and Journal Prompts:
What did you learn about Ben Franklin from reading this book?
Why did the author write this book?
Did the story setting change or stay the same?
Activities for Differentiated Instruction:
Create a board game about the book.
Create a famous person bookmark for Ben Franklin and include facts about him.
Create a timeline for the events in the book.

From *Differentiating Reading Instructing Using Children's Literature* by Liz Knowles, Ed.D.
Santa Barbara, CA: Libraries Unlimited. Copyright © 2009.

Title: *Spiders*
Author: Nic Bishop
Author Web Site: http://www.nicbishop.com
Publisher: Scholastic
Date: 2007
ISBN #: 0439877563
Genre: Nonfiction
Synopsis: Everything you ever wanted to know about all different kinds of spiders with great photographs and informative text.
Audience: Grades PK–3
Award: Robert F. Sibert Honor Book 2008
Curricular Connections
Topics: Spiders
Discussion Questions and Journal Prompts:
What did you learn about spiders?
Did anything in the book surprise you?
Did the photographs help you to better understand spiders?
Activities for Differentiated Instruction:
Write a poem about a spider (but not Itsy-Bitsy!).
Create a fact chart about spiders for your classroom.
Think of two different exciting titles for the book.

Title: *Starring Miss Darlene*
Author: Amy Schwartz
Publisher: Roaring Brook Press
Date: 2007
ISBN #: 1596432307
Genre: Fiction
Synopsis: Much to her surprise, the onstage mishaps of an aspiring actress are reviewed favorably by the theater critic.
Audience: Grades K–3
Curricular Connections
Topics: Actors/Actresses, Hippopotamus, Humorous Stories, Theater
Discussion Questions and Journal Prompts:
What makes this story funny?
Would you like to act in the theater? Why or why not?
What do you know about a hippopotamus?
Activities for Differentiated Instruction:
Act out a part of the story for your classmates.
Write a brief review of a performance you have seen recently.
Draw a poster about this book.

Title: *The Planet Hunter: How Astronomer Mike Brown's Search for the 10th Planet Shook Up the Solar System*
Author: Elizabeth Rusch
Author Web Site: http://www.elizabethrusch.com
Publisher: Rising Moon
Date: 2007
ISBN #: 0873589262
Genre: Nonfiction—Biography
Synopsis: This book tells the story of astronomer Mike Brown, from his childhood and his love for the planets to his amazing discoveries as an adult.
Audience: Grades 2–4
Curricular Connections
Topics: Astronomy, Dwarf Planet, Pluto
Discussion Questions and Journal Prompts:
What did you learn about the planets from this book?
What has happened to Pluto?
Would you like to be an astronomer? Why or why not?
Activities for Differentiated Instruction:
Select one of the planets and create a brief fact chart about it.
Draw the solar system and label the planets.
Create a brief TV news report about the 10th planet.

Title: *The Wolves Are Back*
Author: Jean Craighead George
Author Web Site: http://www.jeancraigheadgeorge.com
Publisher: Dutton Children's Books
Date: 2008
ISBN #: 1430105909
Genre: Nonfiction
Synopsis: For over a century, wolves were persecuted in the United States and nearly became extinct. Gradually reintroduced, they are thriving again in the West, much to the benefit of the ecosystem.
Audience: Grades 1–4
Curricular Connections
Topics: Endangered Species, Reintroduction, Wolves, Yellowstone National Park
Discussion Questions and Journal Prompts:
What does "endangered species" mean?
Why would the ecosystem improve because of wolves?
What did you learn about wolves from this book?
Activities for Differentiated Instruction:
Look at the author's Web site and tell your classmates about her.
Create a poster about wolves.
Write an acrostic about wolves.

From *Differentiating Reading Instructing Using Children's Literature* by Liz Knowles, Ed.D.
Santa Barbara, CA: Libraries Unlimited. Copyright © 2009.

Title: *There Is a Bird on Your Head*
Author: Mo Willems
Author Web Site: http://www.mowillems.com
Publisher: Hyperion
Date: 2007
ISBN #: 1423106865
Genre: Fiction
Synopsis: Gerald the elephant discovers that there is something worse than a bird on your head—two birds on your head! Piggie will try to help her best friend.
Audience: Grades PK–3
Award: Theodor Seuss Geisel Award Winner 2008
Curricular Connections
Topics: Elephants and Pigs, Friends
Discussion Questions and Journal Prompts:
What did you learn about friendship from this book?
What question would you ask the author about the story?
What happened in the story that made you laugh?
Activities for Differentiated Instruction:
Draw a picture from the book and write a sentence to explain it.
Make a bird hat to wear on your head and tell your classmates about the story.
Write a silly poem about the story.

Title: *Those Shoes*
Author: Maribeth Boelts
Author Web Site: http://www.maribethboelts.com
Publisher: Candlewick Press
Date: 2007
ISBN #: 08763624993
Genre: Fiction
Synopsis: Jeremy, who longs to have the black high tops that everyone at school seems to have but his grandmother cannot afford, is excited when he sees them for sale in a thrift shop and decides to buy them, even though they are the wrong size.
Audience: Grades K–3
Curricular Connections
Topics: Generosity, Grandmothers, Poverty, Shoes
Discussion Questions and Journal Prompts:
What have you wanted but could not have?
Why is it important to have shoes that fit properly?
What can you tell about Jeremy from the story?
Activities for Differentiated Instruction:
Write a letter to your friend telling about the story.
Create an acrostic about grandmothers.
Change the name of the story—think of two possible titles.

From *Differentiating Reading Instructing Using Children's Literature* by Liz Knowles, Ed.D.
Santa Barbara, CA: Libraries Unlimited. Copyright © 2009.

Title: *Vulture View*
Author: April Pulley Sayre
Author Web Site: http://www.aprilsayre.com
Publisher: Henry Holt & Company
Date: 2007
ISBN #: 0805075577
Genre: Nonfiction
Synopsis: Turkey vultures do not hunt or kill their food. They eat animals that are already dead, and in this way they provide an important cleaning service in the world of ecology.
Audience: Grades PK–3
Award: Theodor Seuss Geisel Award Honor Book 2008
Curricular Connections
Topics: Ecology, Vultures, Zoology
Discussion Questions and Journal Prompts:
Have you ever seen a turkey vulture?
Why are turkey vultures like a cleaning service?
Would you recommend this book to your classmates? Why or why not?
Activities for Differentiated Instruction:
Make a list of all the good things you can think of about turkey vultures.
Make a business card for a turkey vulture cleaning business—think of a good slogan.
Look at the author's Web site and find something interesting to tell your classmates about her.

Title: *We're Sailing Down The Nile: A Journey through Egypt*
Author: Laurie Krebs
Author Web Site: http://www.lauriekrebs.com
Publisher: Barefoot Books
Date: 2007
ISBN #: 184686194
Genre: Fiction
Synopsis: As the riverboat sails down the Nile River, remnants of Egypt's long history and aspects of its present culture are revealed on its banks. Includes endnotes with additional information about ancient Egyptian culture.
Audience: Grades K–3
Curricular Connections
Topics: Egypt, Nile River, Travel
Discussion Questions and Journal Prompts:
What did you learn about Egypt from this book?
Did the illustrations help you to better understand the history?
Describe the Nile River.
Activities for Differentiated Instruction:
Draw something from Egypt's history. Label it.
Read an interesting part of the book to your classmates.
Create a timeline of events in Egypt's history as explained in the book.

From *Differentiating Reading Instructing Using Children's Literature* by Liz Knowles, Ed.D.
Santa Barbara, CA: Libraries Unlimited. Copyright © 2009.

Title: *You Read to Me, I'll Read to You: Very Short Scary Tales to Read Together*
Author: Mary Ann Hoberman
Author Web Site: http://www.maryannhoberman.com
Publisher: Little, Brown and Company
Date: 2007
ISBN #: 0316017336
Genre: Fiction—Picture Book
Synopsis: Uses alliteration, rhyme, and repetition to invite children to read along with peers or with an adult. Spooky tales of witches, ghosts, and goblins.
Audience: Grades K–3
Curricular Connections
Topics: Poetry, Scary Tales
Discussion Questions and Journal Prompts:
What did you like about this book?
Did the pictures make you scared? Why or why not?
Who was your favorite character?
Activities for Differentiated Instruction:
Draw a picture from the story and write a sentence about it.
Make a list of ten nouns you can find in the book.
Create a greeting card to send to a character in the book.

Lesson Plans Grades 4–7

Title: *Albert Einstein: A Biography*
Author: Milton Meltzer
Publisher: Holiday House
Date: 2008
ISBN #: 0823419661
Genre: Biography
Synopsis: Briefly explores the life of the famous physicist, who was also a peace activist and fighter for social justice.
Audience: Grades 3–6
Curricular Connections
Topics: Albert Einstein, Physicists
Discussion Questions and Journal Prompts:
How is Albert Einstein remembered?
What is a physicist?
What kind of person was Albert Einstein?
Activities for Differentiated Instruction:
Create a 10-word crossword puzzle from story words.
Write three questions about the book for the author.
Construct a timeline of events in Albert Einstein's life.

Title: *Brendan Buckley's Universe and Everything in It*
Author: Sundee Frazier
Author Web Site: http://www.sundeefrazier.com/
Publisher: Delacorte Books for Young Readers
Date: 2007
ISBN #: 044042206X
Genre: Realistic Fiction
Synopsis: Brendan Buckley, a biracial ten-year-old, applies his scientific problem-solving ability and newfound interest in rocks and minerals to connect with his white grandfather, the president of Puyallup Rock Club, and to learn why he and Brendan's mother are estranged.
Audience: Grades 4–8
Award: Coretta Scott King/John Steptoe New Talent Winner—Author Award 2008
Curricular Connections
Topics: Prejudice, Racism
Discussion Questions and Journal Prompts:
What did you learn from reading this book that you had not thought of before?
What is the most important relationship in this story?
At the end of the book did you feel hope for Brendan? Explain.
Activities for Differentiated Instruction:
Do some research on rocks and minerals as a hobby and share the information with your classmates.
Look at the author's Web site and create a poster for the book.
Write a brief epilogue for the story.

From *Differentiating Reading Instructing Using Children's Literature* by Liz Knowles, Ed.D.
Santa Barbara, CA: Libraries Unlimited. Copyright © 2009.

Title: *Chicken Feathers*
Author: Joy Cowley
Author Web Site: http://www.joycowley.com
Publisher: Philomel Books
Date: 2008
ISBN #: 0399247912
Genre: Fiction
Synopsis: Relates the story of the summer when Josh's mother is in the hospital awaiting the birth of his baby sister, and his pet chicken, Semolina, who talks only to him, is almost killed by a red fox.
Audience: Grades 3–5
Curricular Connections
Topics: Farm Life, Chickens, Pets
Discussion Questions and Journal Prompts:
Was the author able to involve you emotionally in the story?
What was the main issue or dilemma in the story?
Was the ending what you expected? Explain.
Activities for Differentiated Instruction:
Draw a picture of Semolina and write a one-sentence description.
Write a letter to the author about the book.
Select a quote or part of a quote from the book and make it into an illustrated poster.

Title: *Come Look with Me: Latin American Art*
Author: Kimberly Lane
Publisher: Charlesbridge
Date: 2007
ISBN #: 1890674206
Genre: Nonfiction
Synopsis: Allows children to interact with and develop a greater understanding of Latin American art through colorful reproductions, brief biographies, and criticism of the artists and questions that facilitate conversation.
Audience: Grades 3–6
Curricular Connections
Topics: Artwork, Latin America
Discussion Questions and Journal Prompts:
What did you like best about the art in the book?
Were the questions provided in the book useful?
Did you learn something from reading this book? If so, what?
Activities for Differentiated Instruction:
Create an award for this book including a medal and a statement for the newspaper.
Select one of the artists and do an Internet search and create a timeline of the artist's life.
Create a crossword using the names and information about the artists in the book.

Title: *Diary of a Wimpy Kid: Rodrick Rules*
Author: Jeff Kinney
Author Web Site: http://www.wimpykid.com
Publisher: Abrams/Amulet Books
Date: 2008
ISBN #: 0810994739
Genre: Fiction
Synopsis: Greg Heffley tells about his summer vacation and his attempts to steer clear of trouble when he returns to middle school and tries to keep his older brother Rodrick from telling everyone about Greg's most humiliating experience of the summer.
Audience: Grades 4–8
Curricular Connections
Topics: Diaries, Families, Middle School
Discussion Questions and Journal Prompts:
Do any of the characters in the book remind you of people you know?
Have you read a story similar to this one? If so, which story?
Describe a time when you were embarrassed by a relative or a friend.
Activities for Differentiated Instruction:
Create questions you would use in an author interview.
Create a marketing slogan for the book.
Design a bookmark for the book.

Title: *Down the Colorado: John Wesley Powell, the One-Armed Explorer*
Author: Deborah Kogan Ray
Author Web Site: http://www.dkray.com
Publisher: Farrar, Straus & Giroux/Frances Foster Books
Date: 2007
ISBN #: 0374318387
Genre: Biography—Picture Book
Synopsis: This is the story of John Wesley Powell, whose Colorado River explorations made him a national hero. Beautiful illustrations trace his life from childhood and scenes from his explorations.
Audience: Grades 3–5
Curricular Connections
Topics: Colorado River, Discovery and Exploration, Explorers—Western US, John Wesley Powell—1834–1902
Discussion Questions and Journal Prompts:
What do you think it felt like to be an explorer in the late 1800s?
What did you learn from reading this book?
What would you have done differently if you were exploring the Colorado River?
Activities for Differentiated Instruction:
Create a historical timeline of the events in this book.
Create a travel brochure for the Colorado River.
Adapt the story for a movie.

From *Differentiating Reading Instructing Using Children's Literature* by Liz Knowles, Ed.D.
Santa Barbara, CA: Libraries Unlimited. Copyright © 2009.

Title: *Elijah of Buxton*
Author: Christopher Paul Curtis
Author Web Site: http://www.randomhouse.com/features/christopherpaulcurtis/
Publisher: Scholastic
Date: 2007
ISBN #: 0439023440
Genre: Historical Fiction
Synopsis: In 1859, eleven-year-old Elijah Freeman, the first freeborn child in Buxton, Canada, which is a haven for slaves fleeing the American South, uses his wits and skills to try to bring to justice the lying preacher who has stolen money that was to be used to buy a family's freedom.
Audience: Grades 4–7
Awards: Newbery Medal Honor Book Winner 2008
Coretta Scott King Author Award Winner 2008
Curricular Connections:
Topics: African-Canadian, Multicultural, Slavery
Discussion Questions and Journal Prompts:
What kind of person was Elijah? Describe his characteristics.
What was the theme of this story?
Did the book's cover art add to or detract from the story? Explain.
Activities for Differentiated Instruction:
Create an acrostic for this story using the word "freedom."
Design a bookmark for the book.
Research Buxton, Canada. Write about the history with regard to slaves and the United States.

Title: *Face to Face with Dolphins*
Author: Flip and Linda Nicklin
Publisher: National Geographic Children's Books
Date: 2007
ISBN #: 1426301413
Genre: Nonfiction
Synopsis: Written and photographed by Flip Nicklin, a *National Geographic* photographer and his wife, Linda, an educator and a naturalist, this book allows readers to see these gentle creatures close up. The book hopes to generate interest, compassion, and concern for these beautiful and friendly underwater mammals.
Audience: Grades 3–6
Curricular Connections
Topics: Conservation, Dolphins, Marine Animal Care, Marine Environments, Photography
Discussion Questions and Journal Prompts:
In what way did the photos add to the story?
What did you learn about dolphins from reading this book?
Why do you think it is important to take care of marine environments?
Activities for Differentiated Instruction:
Create a diorama of a marine environment where dolphins might live.
Do some additional research on dolphins and share the information with the class.
Write a poem about dolphins and the sea.

Title: *First the Egg*
Author: Laura Vaccaro Seeger
Author Web Site: http://www.studiolvs.com
Publisher: Roaring Brook Press
Date: 2007
ISBN #: 1596432721
Genre: Nonfiction
Synopsis: This story explores the question, which comes first, the chicken or the egg.
Audience: Grades 4–8
Awards: Caldecott Medal Honor Book 2008; Theodor Seuss Geisel Honor Book 2008
Curricular Connections:
Topics: Biology, Nature—Basic Concepts, Science
Discussion Questions and Journal Prompts:
After reading the book, is it true? Did the egg come first?
What useful information, if any, did the book provide?
Share some information about the author with your classmates.
Activities for Differentiated Instruction:
Make a word-search puzzle with words from the story.
Create a newspaper headline and brief story about the book.
Make a four-slide computer presentation about the author and the book.

Title: *Four Feet, Two Sandals*
Author: Karen Lynn Williams & Khadra Mohammed
Author Web Site: http://www.karenlynnwilliams.com
Publisher: Eerdmans Books for Young Readers
Date: 2007
ISBN #: 0802582963
Genre: Fiction
Synopsis: Two young Afghani girls, living in a refugee camp in Pakistan, share a precious pair of sandals brought by relief workers.
Audience: Grades 2–5
Curricular Connections
Topics: Pakistan, Refugee Camps, Sharing, Shoes
Discussion Questions and Journal Prompts:
What was the theme of this story?
What was your favorite part of the story?
What surprised you about this story?
Activities for Differentiated Instruction:
Draw a map of Pakistan and write a brief description of the country.
Write a newspaper report about the refugee camp.
Read aloud a passage from the book to your classmates.

From *Differentiating Reading Instructing Using Children's Literature* by Liz Knowles, Ed.D.
Santa Barbara, CA: Libraries Unlimited. Copyright © 2009.

Title: *Hurt Go Happy*
Author: Ginny Rorby
Author Web Site: http://www.ginnyrorby.com
Publisher: Starscape
Date: 2007
ISBN #: 0765353040
Genre: Realistic Fiction
Synopsis: When thirteen-year-old Joey Willis, deaf since the age of six, meets Dr. Charles Mansell and his chimpanzee Sukari, who use sign language, her world blooms with possibilities.
Audience: Grades 4–7
Curricular Connections
Topics: Animals, Apes and Monkeys, Deafness
Discussion Questions and Journal Prompts:
What kind of a person was Joey?
What did you find to be unusual about the story?
Would you recommend the book to a friend? Why or why not?
Activities for Differentiated Instruction:
Write an article for a newspaper about chimpanzees and sign language.
Create an ad for a children's magazine about the book.
Learn to say three things in sign language and share them with your classmates.

Title: *In the Land of the Jaguar: South America and Its People*
Author: Gena K. Gorrell
Author Web Site: http://www.genagorrellbooks.org
Publisher: Tundra Books
Date: 2007
ISBN #: 0887767567
Genre: Nonfiction
Synopsis: Journey to the extraordinary lands that make up the continent of South America.
Audience: Grades 5–7
Curricular Connections
Topics: Animals, Customs, History, South America, Travel
Discussion Questions and Journal Prompts:
What did you learn from this book?
What South American country would you most like to visit? Explain.
Why do you think the author wrote this book? Look at the Web site.
Activities for Differentiated Instruction:
Design a travel brochure for one of the South American countries.
Do some research and write a report about the jaguar.
Create a board game about South America.

Title: *Invention of Hugo Cabret*
Author: Brian Selznick
Author Web Site: http://www.theinventionofhugocabret.com
Publisher: Scholastic
Date: 2007
ISBN #: 0439813786
Genre: Historical Fiction
Synopsis: When twelve-year-old Hugo, an orphan living and repairing clocks, within the walls of a Paris train station in 1931, meets a mysterious toy seller and his goddaughter, his undercover life and his biggest secret are jeopardized.
Audience: Grades 4–7
Award: Caldecott Medal Winner 2008
Curricular Connections:
Topics: Europe, Foster Homes, Orphans
Discussion Questions and Journal Prompts:
What was Hugo's secret?
What surprised you about the story?
What do you know about foster homes and orphanages?
Activities for Differentiated Instruction:
Write a letter to the author about the book.
Make a collage of pictures of clocks and watches cut from magazines.
Look at the Web site and create a poster about the author and the book.

Title: *Lenny's Space*
Author: Kate Banks
Publisher: Farrar, Straus & Giroux/Frances Foster Books
Date: 2007
ISBN #: 0374345759
Genre: Realistic Fiction
Synopsis: Nine-year-old Lenny gets in trouble and has no friends because he cannot control himself in school and his interests are not like those of his classmates, until he starts visiting Muriel, a counselor, and meets Van, a boy his age who has leukemia.
Audience: Grades 3–5
Curricular Connections
Topics: Counselors, Friendship, Leukemia, Single-Parent Families
Discussion Questions and Journal Prompts:
Why is friendship an important part of this story?
What does Lenny learn from Van?
If you were the author, how would you change the story?
Activities for Differentiated Instruction:
Write an investigative report on leukemia for a medical column in a newspaper.
Write an illustrated poem about friendship.
Prepare questions you would ask if you were going to interview the author.

From *Differentiating Reading Instructing Using Children's Literature* by Liz Knowles, Ed.D.
Santa Barbara, CA: Libraries Unlimited. Copyright © 2009.

Title: *Martina the Beautiful Cockroach: A Cuban Folktale*
Author: Carmen Agra Deedy
Author Web Site: http://carmendeedy.com/
Publisher: Peachtree
Date: 2007
ISBN #: 1561453994
Genre: Fairy Tale
Synopsis: In this humorous retelling of a Cuban folktale, a cockroach interviews her suitors in order to decide whom to marry.
Audience: Grades 4–7
Awards: Pura Belpre Award Honor Book 2008
Curricular Connections
Topics: Cockroaches, Folktales, Multicultural
Discussion Questions and Journal Prompts:
What makes this story humorous?
What other folktales have you read?
What do you know about Cuba?
Activities for Differentiated Instruction:
Write questions for the cockroach about her choice.
Create a short folktale about another kind of bug.
Write an illustrated poem about a cockroach.

Title: *Mysteries of the Mummy Kids*
Author: Kelly Milner Halls
Author Web Site: http://www.kellymilnerhalls.com
Publisher: Darby Creek Publishing
Date: 2007
ISBN #: 158196059X
Genre: Nonfiction
Synopsis: The story, with pictures, of mummified children from as long ago as 7,000 years up to a Civil War child found in 2005. It includes interviews with mummy finders, scientists, and a modern-day embalmer.
Audience: Grades 4–8
Curricular Connections
Topics: Embalmers, Mummies, Scientists
Discussion Questions and Journal Prompts:
What kind of research did the author have to do to write this book?
What did you learn from this book?
What part of the story surprised you?
Activities for Differentiated Instruction:
Go to the author's Web site and share information about her with your classmates.
Create a ten-word crossword from the story.
Write a five-question test for the book. Give it to a classmate who has read the book.

Title: *Our Liberty Bell*
Author: Henry Jonas Magaziner
Publisher: Holiday House
Date: 2007
ISBN #: 0823420817
Genre: Nonfiction
Synopsis: In 1752, the Liberty Bell was first used in Philadelphia to gather the people for news about the Revolutionary War. This book tells the entire story of the bell.
Audience: Grades 4–6
Curricular Connections
Topics: Liberty Bell, Philadelphia
Discussion Questions and Journal Prompts:
What questions would you ask the author?
What did you learn about the Liberty Bell from the book?
What did you like about the organization of the information in the book?
Activities for Differentiated Instruction:
Make an acrostic for the words "Liberty Bell" with words from the book.
Write a travel ad for Philadelphia during the late 1700s using ideas from the book.
Make a drawing of the Liberty Bell, mount it on tag, and cut it out to make a puzzle.

Title: *Reaching for Sun*
Author: Tracie Vaughn Zimmer
Author Web Site: http://www.tracievaughnzimmer.com
Publisher: Bloomsberry USA
Date: 2007
ISBN #: 1599900378
Genre: Realistic Fiction
Synopsis: Josie, who lives with her mother and grandmother and has cerebral palsy, befriends a boy who moves into one of the rich houses behind her old farmhouse.
Audience: Grades 4–7
Award: Schneider Family Book Award—Middle School
Curricular Connections
Topics: Cerebral Palsy
Discussion Questions and Journal Prompts:
What kind of a person was Josie?
What challenges did she face with her disability?
What can you learn from this story?
Activities for Differentiated Instruction:
Write an investigative report about cerebral palsy for a newspaper.
Look at the author's Web site and create a board game about her and her books.
Create an eight-word crossword about the book.

From *Differentiating Reading Instructing Using Children's Literature* by Liz Knowles, Ed.D.
Santa Barbara, CA: Libraries Unlimited. Copyright © 2009.

Title: *Silent Music*
Author: James Rumford
Author Web Site: http://www.houghtonmifflinbooks.com/catalog/authordetail.cfm?authorID=1388
Publisher: Roaring Brook/A Neal Porter Book
Date: 2008
ISBN #: 1596432764
Genre: Fiction
Synopsis: As bombs and missiles fall on Baghdad in 2003, a young boy uses the art of calligraphy to distance himself from the horror of war.
Audience: Grades 2–6
Curricular Connections
Topics: Arabic, Baghdad, Calligraphy, Iraq War 2003
Discussion Questions and Journal Prompts:
What challenges did Ali have to face in Baghdad?
What word did Ali have trouble writing? How was that strange?
What were Ali's other favorite things to do besides calligraphy?
Activities for Differentiated Instruction:
Draw the word "peace" in calligraphy and create an illustration to accompany it.
Write a report for *Time Magazine* about the 2003 Baghdad War.
Create a bookmark for the book.

Title: *Sneeze!*
Author: Alexandra Siy
Author Web Site: http://www.alexandrasiy.com
Publisher: Charlesbridge
Date: 2007
ISBN #: 1570916543
Genre: Nonfiction—Picture Book
Synopsis: Explains the causes of sneezing.
Audience: Grades 4–6
Curricular Connections
Topics: Sneezing
Discussion Questions and Journal Prompts:
What did you learn about sneezing that you did not already know?
When you go to sneeze next time, will you do something different?
What would you ask the author?
Activities for Differentiated Instruction:
Review the author's Web site and create an ad for a children's magazine about her and her books.
Write a report about sneezing for a medical column in a newspaper.
Make a poster about the book with a nose and some tissue and important information about sneezing.

Title: *Tap Dancing on the Roof*
Author: Linda Sue Park
Author Web Site: http://www.lspark.com
Publisher: Clarion Books
Date: 2007
ISBN #: 0618234837
Genre: Poetry
Synopsis: Sijo is a traditional poetry form from Korea—similar to Japanese Haiku. There are 26 in this collection, some humorous but all geared for children to enjoy.
Audience: Grades 2–6
Curricular Connections
Topics: Korea, Poetry, Sijo
Discussion Questions and Journal Prompts:
What do you know about Haiku? How is it different from Sijo?
What was unusual about this kind of poetry?
What theme was expressed through the poetry?
Activities for Differentiated Instruction:
Create an illustrated Korean Sijo poem.
Create an illustrated Japanese Haiku poem.
Read some Sijo examples from the book to your classmates.

Title: *The Buddha's Diamonds*
Author: Carolyn Marsden and Thay Phap Niem
Author Web Site: http://www.carolynmarsden.com
Publisher: Candlewick Press
Date: 2008
ISBN #: 0763633806
Genre: Fiction
Synopsis: As a storm sweeps in, Tinh's father tells him to tie up their fishing boat, but the storm scares him and he runs away. When the damage to the boat is discovered, Tinh realizes what he must do.
Audience: Grades 4–7
Curricular Connections
Topics: Fishers, Responsibility, Vietnam
Discussion Questions and Journal Prompts:
What did this story tell you about responsibility?
Why was their fishing boat so important to this family?
What surprised you about this story?
Activities for Differentiated Instruction:
Create a travel brochure for Vietnam.
Explore the author's Web site. Share several interesting things about her with your classmates.
Create a five-word crossword puzzle about the story.

From *Differentiating Reading Instructing Using Children's Literature* by Liz Knowles, Ed.D. Santa Barbara, CA: Libraries Unlimited. Copyright © 2009.

Title: *The Down-to-Earth Guide to Global Warming*
Author: Laurie David and Cambria Gordon
Author Web Site: http://www.lauriedavid.com
Publisher: Scholastic/Orchard Books
Date: 2007
ISBN #: 0439024943
Genre: Nonfiction
Synopsis: Describes why global warming happens, how it affects the planet, and measures that can be taken to stop it.
Audience: Grades 4–6
Curricular Connections
Topics: Global Warming
Discussion Questions and Journal Prompts:
What were a few things you learned about global warming from this book?
What did you read in the book that surprised you?
What can you do to make a difference?
Activities for Differentiated Instruction:
Investigate the author's Web site and create a poster about the author or about the book or about global warming trends and issues.
Create a fact sheet to share with your classmates with information about global warming from the book.
Make a TV ad (like a public service announcement) to alert kids about what can be done.

Title: *The Girls Like Spaghetti: Why, You Can't Manage without Apostrophes!*
Author: Lynne Truss
Author Web Site: http://www.lynnetruss.com
Publisher: G. P. Putnam's Sons
Date: 2007
ISBN #: 0399247068
Genre: Nonfiction—Picture Book
Synopsis: See how using (or not using) an apostrophe can change the meaning of a sentence.
Audience: Grades 2–5
Curricular Connections
Topics: English Language, Punctuation
Discussion Questions and Journal Prompts:
What did you learn about apostrophes?
What did you find to be amusing about this book?
Will this help you to use apostrophes correctly? Explain.
Activities for Differentiated Instruction:
Make a chart listing five types of punctuation, telling how each is used, and giving an example.
Write a sequel to this story. What other form of punctuation can't you live without?
Explore the author's Web site and then make a poster about the book.

Title: *The Moon Is La Luna: Silly Rhymes in English and Spanish*
Author: Jay M. Harris
Publisher: Houghton Mifflin
Date: 2007
ISBN #: 0618646450
Genre: Fiction
Synopsis: Easy-to-read text introduces Spanish words and rhymes them with English words that are sometimes very different as well as providing advice on using words that are much the same.
Audience: Grades 4–6
Curricular Connections
Topics: Humor, Rhymes, Spanish
Discussion Questions and Journal Prompts:
What did you learn from this book?
What was the author trying to accomplish by writing this book?
Did the illustrations add to the story? Explain.
Activities for Differentiated Instruction:
Create a ten-word Spanish dictionary with words and illustrations.
Write a letter to a friend about this book.
Create an ad for this book for a children's magazine.

Title: *The Perfect Catsitter*
Author: Ann Nagda
Author Web Site: http://www.annnagda.com
Publisher: Holiday House
Date: 2007
ISBN #: 0823421120
Genre: Fiction
Synopsis: When her friend Rana goes to India, Susan volunteers to take care of her cat and her sister's fish, but the job turns out to be much more difficult than she expected.
Audience: Grades 3–4
Curricular Connections
Topics: Cats, Pet Sitting, School
Discussion Questions and Journal Prompts:
What surprised you about this story?
What kind of a friend was Susan?
What do you know about cat sitting?
Activities for Differentiated Instruction:
Create a business card and flyer for your cat-sitting business.
Visit the author's Web site. You can see why she wrote about cats! Print out some bookmarks that are available there and share them with your friends.
Write a letter to the author about her books.

From *Differentiating Reading Instructing Using Children's Literature* by Liz Knowles, Ed.D.
Santa Barbara, CA: Libraries Unlimited. Copyright © 2009.

Title: *The Seer of Shadows*
Author: Avi
Author Web Site: http://www.avi-writer.com
Publisher: HarperCollins
Date: 2008
ISBN #: 0060000155
Genre: Fiction
Synopsis: In New York City in 1872, fourteen-year-old Horace, a photographer's apprentice, becomes entangled in a plot to create fraudulent spirit photographs, but when Horace accidentally frees the real ghost of a dead girl bent on revenge, his life takes a frightening turn.
Audience: Grades 4–6
Curricular Connections
Topics: Ghosts, Horror Stories, Photography, Revenge, Swindlers
Discussion Questions and Journal Prompts:
Avi says on his Web site, "I want my readers to feel, to think, sometimes to laugh. But most of all I want them to enjoy a good read." Did he accomplish that with this book?
What part of the story was the most frightening?
What did you learn about Horace from reading this story?
Activities for Differentiated Instruction:
Create a four-frame comic strip to tell this story.
Write an epilogue to this story.
Read a portion of this story to a classmate.

Title: *The Strongest Man in the World*
Author: Nicolas Debon
Publisher: Groundwood Books
Date: 2007
ISBN #: 0888997310
Genre: Biography—Picture Book
Synopsis: This is the life story of strong man Louis Cyr told by him from his old-age vantage point. He was a circus owner in Quebec in the early twentieth century.
Audience: Grades 2–5
Curricular Connections
Topics: Circus, Performing Arts
Discussion Questions and Journal Prompts:
What did you learn about the life of a circus performer?
If you were a circus performer, what would you do?
How is the circus different today?
Activities for Differentiated Instruction:
Make a poster advertising the circus described in the book.
Pretend you are the ringmaster for this circus; announce the strongman's act.
Make a ten-word crossword of circus words.

Title: *The Year of the Rat*
Author: Grace Lin
Author Web Site: http://www.gracelin.com
Publisher: Little, Brown and Company
Date: 2008
ISBN #: 0316033618
Genre: Fiction
Synopsis: In the Chinese Year of the Rat, a young Taiwanese American girl faces many challenges: her best friend moves to California and a new boy comes to her school, she must find the courage to forge ahead with her dream of becoming a writer and illustrator, and she must learn to find the beauty in change.
Audience: Grades 3–5
Curricular Connections
Topics: Chinese New Year, Family Life, Identity, Schools, Taiwanese Americans
Discussion Questions and Journal Prompts:
What did you learn about the Chinese New Year celebration from this book?
What do you dream of becoming?
What surprised you about this book?
Activities for Differentiated Instruction:
Go to the author's Web site and spend some time there—lots to do and see!
Create a brightly colored poster to advertise the book.
Make a board game with facts about Chinese culture.

Title: *Twelve Rounds to Glory: The Story of Muhammad Ali*
Author: Charles R. Smith, Jr.
Author Web Site: http://www.charlesrsmithjr.com/
Publisher: Candlewick Press
Date: 2007
ISBN #: 0763616923
Genre: Nonfiction—Biography
Synopsis: A brief biography in verse of boxer Muhammad Ali.
Audience: Grades 4–7
Award: Coretta Scott King Author Award Honor Book 2008
Curricular Connections:
Topics: Biography, Boxing, Multicultural, Sports
Discussion Questions and Journal Prompts:
What was Muhammad Ali's most famous line?
What did you learn about Muhammad Ali from this book?
What did you learn about the sport of boxing from reading this book?
Activities for Differentiated Instruction:
Check out the author's Web site—you can listen to him read a poem from the book.
Research a current boxer and write a paragraph about him.
Create a brief review of this book for a newspaper's sports column.

From *Differentiating Reading Instructing Using Children's Literature* by Liz Knowles, Ed.D.
Santa Barbara, CA: Libraries Unlimited. Copyright © 2009.

Title: *United Tweets of America*
Author: Hudson Talbott
Author Web Site: http://www.hudsontalbott.com
Publisher: G. P. Putnam's Sons
Date: 2008
ISBN #: 0399245200
Genre: Nonfiction
Synopsis: Learn the nickname and state bird for each state, plus other state trivia.
Audience: Grades 1–4
Curricular Connections
Topics: State Birds, States
Discussion Questions and Journal Prompts:
What did you learn about the bird from your state?
Which bird do you think deserved to be the Top Tweet and why?
What did you think of the illustrations? Explain.
Activities for Differentiated Instruction:
Write a poem about the bird that represents your state.
Write a letter about the book to the author.
Draw a bookmark for the book.

Title: *Wall: Growing Up behind the Iron Curtain*
Author: Peter Sis
Author Web Site: http://www.petersis.com
Publisher: Farrar, Straus & Giroux
Date: 2007
ISBN #: 0374347018
Genre: Biography
Synopsis: Journal entries, photos, and historical facts tell the story of the life of Peter Sis, who grew up in Prague during the Cold War.
Audience: Grades 4–7
Awards: Caldecott Medal Honor Book 2008; Robert F. Sibert Award Winner 2008
Curricular Connections:
Topics: Art—Painting
Discussion Questions and Journal Prompts:
What did you learn about Peter Sis?
What kind of person was Peter Sis? Describe his character traits.
What did you learn from the book?
Activities for Differentiated Instruction:
Look at the author's Web site and create a poster about him and his books.
Write a letter to Peter Sis about this book.
Illustrate a scene from the book and write a brief description.

Title: *When Harriet Met Sojourner*
Author: Catherine Clinton
Author Web Site: http://www.catherineclinton.com/
Publisher: HarperCollins/Katherine Tegen Books
Date: 2007
ISBN #: 0060504250
Genre: Nonfiction
Synopsis: Harriet Tubman and Sojourner Truth, both former slaves, met for the first time in 1864 and worked tirelessly together for the future of African American women.
Audience: Grades 3-7
Curricular Connections
Topics: African American Women, Harriet Tubman, Slaves, Social Reformers, Sojourner Truth
Discussion Questions and Journal Prompts:
What is the theme of the book?
What was the author's purpose for writing this book?
What information in the book changed the way you think? Explain.
Activities for Differentiated Instruction:
Create a bumper sticker to advertise this book.
Create a board game using facts from the book.
Write a three-entry diary for one of the characters.

Title: *When Is a Planet Not a Planet?: The Story of Pluto*
Author: Elaine Scott
Author Web Site: http://www.elainescott.com
Publisher: Clarion Books
Date: 2007
ISBN #: 0618898328
Genre: Nonfiction
Synopsis: This book tells about the wanderers, some early astronomers, ideas that work—and those that don't, Pluto's problems, finding planets, and answers the question, what is a planet?
Audience: Grades 3–6
Curricular Connections
Topics: Dwarf Planet, Pluto
Discussion Questions and Journal Prompts:
What did you learn about the planets from this book?
What did you find out about the current status of Pluto?
How helpful were the drawings and illustrations?
Activities for Differentiated Instruction:
Look at the author's Web site—she has a new book about life on Mars. Get it and find out if she thinks there is or isn't!
Draw a poster to advertise the book.
Create a ten-word crossword with information from the book.

From *Differentiating Reading Instructing Using Children's Literature* by Liz Knowles, Ed.D.
Santa Barbara, CA: Libraries Unlimited. Copyright © 2009.

Title: *Why War Is Never a Good Idea*
Author: Alice Walker
Author Web Site: http://aalbc.com/authors/alice.htm
Publisher: HarperCollins
Date: 2007
ISBN #: 0060753854
Genre: Poetry
Synopsis: Simple rhythmic text explores the wanton destructiveness of war, which has grown old but not wise as it demolishes nice people and beautiful things with no consideration for the consequences.
Audience: Grades 3 and up
Curricular Connections
Topics: Poetry, War
Discussion Questions and Journal Prompts:
How do the illustrations add to this story?
What surprised you about this story?
What does the author want you to do?
Activities for Differentiated Instruction:
Create a news story for a newspaper about the book.
Draw a poster to tell about the book.
Create an acrostic about war and its deadly results.

Lesson Plans for Young Adults

Title: *Big Fat Manifesto*
Author: Susan Vaught
Author Web Site: http://www.susanvaught.com
Publisher: Bloomsbury USA
Date: 2008
ISBN#: 1599905040
Genre: Fiction
Synopsis: Overweight, self-assured, high school senior Jamie Carcaterra writes in the school newspaper about her own attitude about being fat, her boyfriend's bariatric surgery, and her struggles to be taken seriously in a very thin world.
Audience: Young Adult
Curricular Connections
Topics: High School, Interpersonal Relationships, Overweight, Prejudice, Self-confidence
Discussion Questions and Journal Prompts:
What makes this story realistic fiction?
Read about the author on her Web site—she was overweight as a child—look at the titles of her books—what does that tell you?
How does this story make you feel?
Activities for Differentiated Instruction:
Research bariatric surgery—is it dangerous?
Create an illustrated, five-entry journal as if you were one of the characters in this story.
Create a poster about self-confidence.

Title: *Chandra's Wars*
Author: Allan Stratton
Author Web Site: http://www.allanstratton.com
Publisher: HarperTeen
Date: 2008
ISBN #: 0060872624
Genre: Fiction
Synopsis: Chandra Kabelo, a teenaged African girl, must save her younger siblings after they are kidnapped and forced to serve as child soldiers in General Mandiki's rebel army.
Audience: Young Adult
Curricular Connections
Topics: Africa, Blacks, Civil War, Kidnapping, Orphans
Discussion Questions and Journal Prompts:
Would reading this story help you to understand our Civil War when you study it in history class?
Which character was most memorable and why?
What did you learn about child soldiers from reading this story?
Activities for Differentiated Instruction:
Write a letter to your best friend about this book.
Make a collage about this book using pictures cut from magazines.
Select three short passages from the book and read them to your classmates.

From *Differentiating Reading Instructing Using Children's Literature* by Liz Knowles, Ed.D.
Santa Barbara, CA: Libraries Unlimited. Copyright © 2009.

Title: *Child of Dandelions*	
Author: Shenaaz Nanji	
Author Web Site: http://www.snanji.com	
Publisher: Front Street	
Date: 2008	
ISBN #: 1932425934	
Genre: Fiction	
Synopsis: In Uganda in 1972, fifteen-year-old Sabine and her family, wealthy citizens of Indian descent, try to preserve their normal life during the ninety days allowed by President Idi Amin for all foreign Indians to leave the country, while soldiers and others terrorize them and people disappear.	
Audience: Young Adult	
Curricular Connections	
Topics: East Indians, Ethnic Relations, Forced Migration, Idi Amin—1925–2003, Uganda	
Discussion Questions and Journal Prompts:	
Why did you select this book? Did it surprise you?	
What was the turning point in this story?	
How is the setting important to the telling of this story?	
Activities for Differentiated Instruction:	
Research this time in history and create a timeline of actual events.	
Prepare a character trait chart of President Idi Amin.	
Make a vocabulary list of ten unusual words from the story and include meanings.	

Title: *Crossing to Paradise*	
Author: Kevin Holland-Crossley	
Author Web Site: http://www.ncbf.org.uk/03/crossley-holland/crossley-holland.html	
Publisher: Scholastic/Arthur A. Levine Books	
Date: 2008	
ISBN #: 054505866X	
Genre: Fiction	
Synopsis: When fifteen-year-old Gatty, an illiterate field-girl who sings beautifully, is selected for a pilgrimage, she travels from her home on an English estate to London, Venice, and eventually Jerusalem, and experiences great changes in her circumstances and in herself.	
Audience: Young Adult	
Curricular Connections	
Topics: Great Britain History, Literacy, Middle Ages, Pilgrims, Singing	
Discussion Questions and Journal Prompts:	
Why do you think the author wrote this story?	
What did you learn from Gatty?	
What images do you remember from the story?	
Activities for Differentiated Instruction:	
Write a *New York Times*–style book review for this story.	
Write three entries for Gatty's diary.	
Create a travel brochure for London, England.	

Title: *Does My Head Look Big in This?*
Author: Randa Abdel-Fattah
Author Web Site: http://www.abc.net.au/queensland/stories/s1437645.htm
Publisher: Scholastic/Orchard
Date: 2007
ISBN #: 043992233X
Genre: Fiction
Synopsis: Year Eleven at an exclusive prep school in the suburbs of Melbourne, Australia, would be tough enough, but it is further complicated for Amal when she has to wear the hijab, the Muslim head scarf, full-time as a badge of her faith—without losing her identity or sense of style.
Audience: Young Adult
Curricular Connections
Topics: Australia, Hijab, Islam, Islamic Customs, Muslims
Discussion Questions and Journal Prompts:
What did you learn from one of the characters in the story?
What are some other ways cultural differences affect students?
Is the title appropriate for the story? Why or why not?
Activities for Differentiated Instruction:
Research the author and create a brief video about her and the book.
Create a crossword puzzle for this book using at least ten words from the story.
Draw a map of Australia showing where Melbourne is located, along with other important places.

Title: *Dreamquake: Book Two of the Dreamhunter Duet*
Author: Elizabeth Knox
Author Web Site: http://us.macmillan.com/author/elizabethknox
Publisher: Farrar, Straus & Giroux
Date: 2007
ISBN #: 0374318543
Genre: Fiction—Fantasy
Synopsis: Aided by her family and her creation, Nown, Laura investigates the powerful Regulatory Body's involvement in mysterious disappearances and activities and learns, in the process, the true nature of the Place in which dreams are found.
Audience: Young Adult
Award: Michael L. Printz Award Honor Book 2008
Curricular Connections
Topics: Dreams, Fantasy
Discussion Questions and Journal Prompts:
What is the significance of dreams in this story?
Which character is the most interesting and why?
Did anything that happened in the story ever happen to you? What?
Activities for Differentiated Instruction:
Adapt this story for a play and share it with your classmates.
Create a character trait graphic organizer focusing on two characters.
Design a bookmark for this book.

From *Differentiating Reading Instructing Using Children's Literature* by Liz Knowles, Ed.D.
Santa Barbara, CA: Libraries Unlimited. Copyright © 2009.

Title: *Feathers*
Author: Jacqueline Woodson
Author Web Site: http://www.jacquelinewoodson.com
Publisher: Putnam Juvenile
Date: 2007
ISBN #: 0399239898
Genre: Realistic Fiction
Synopsis: When a new white student nicknamed "The Jesus Boy" joins her sixth-grade class in the winter of 1971, Frannie's growing friendship with him makes her start to see some things in a new light.
Audience: Young Adult
Award: Newbery Medal Honor Book 2008
Curricular Connections
Topics: Prejudice, Racism, Special Needs
Discussion Questions and Journal Prompts:
Which character did you like the least and why?
Did you feel that you were part of the story or only an observer? Why?
How does the year of the story make it different from a story set in today's times?
Activities for Differentiated Instruction:
Look at the author's Web site and then send her an e-mail about the book.
Create a magazine advertisement for the book.
Draw an illustration from the book.

Title: *Flipped*
Author: Wendelin Van Draanen
Author Web Site: http://www.randomhouse.com/kids/vandraanen/
Publisher: Alfred A. Knopf
Date: 2001
ISBN #: 0375825444
Genre: Realistic Fiction—Relationships and Friendships
Synopsis: In alternating chapters, two teenagers describe how their feelings about themselves, each other, and their families have changed over the years.
Audience: Young Adult
Curricular Connections
Topics: Environmental Issues, Family Life, Interpersonal Relationships
Discussion Questions and Journal Prompts:
What surprises happened in this book?
Did you feel like you were part of the story or an observer?
Have you ever taken a stand for something you believe in?
Activities for Differentiated Instruction:
Write a poem or an acrostic about a friend.
Create a newspaper column where you give advice about friends.
Research environmental issues, being proactive for a cause.

Title: *Forgotten Ellis Island: The Extraordinary Story of America's Immigrant Hospital*
Author: Lorie Conway
Publisher: Smithsonian Books
Date: 2007
ISBN #: 0061241962
Genre: Nonfiction
Synopsis: The story of the construction of the Immigrant Hospital, the thousands of patients treated, and how it fell into disuse and decay.
Audience: Young Adult
Curricular Connections
Topics: Ellis Island Hospital, Emigration/Immigration, Immigrants, New York City, New Jersey History
Discussion Questions and Journal Prompts:
What do you think it was like to come to a new country?
What surprised you about the Immigrant Hospital?
What is Ellis Island like today?
Tell about the photos in the book. Did they add to the understanding of the times?
Activities for Differentiated Instruction:
Draw a scene from the Immigrant Hospital.
Write an interview with an immigrant in the early 1900s.
Create a chart depicting the number of immigrants arriving in the United States from 1900 to 1915.

Title: *Game*
Author: Walter Dean Myers
Author Web Site: http://www.walterdeanmyers.com
Publisher: HarperTeen
Date: 2008
ISBN #: 0060582944
Genre: Fiction
Synopsis: If Harlem high school senior Drew Lawson is going to realize his dream of playing college, and then professional, basketball, he will have to improve at being a team player, especially after a new white student threatens to take the scouts' attention away from him.
Audience: Young Adult
Curricular Connections
Topics: African Americans, Family, Basketball, High School, Teamwork
Discussion Questions and Journal Prompts:
What did you like about the basketball theme of this book?
What experiences have you had that help you understand this book?
If you were the author, how would you have changed the story?
Activities for Differentiated Instruction:
Create an award for the main character.
Go to the author's Web site and then share information about him with your classmates.
Write a newspaper article about this book for the sports section.

From *Differentiating Reading Instructing Using Children's Literature* by Liz Knowles, Ed.D.
Santa Barbara, CA: Libraries Unlimited. Copyright © 2009.

Title: *Good Masters! Sweet Ladies! Voices from a Medieval Village*
Author: Laura Amy Schlitz
Author Web Site: http://www.parkschool.net/more.cfm?objectid=144
Publisher: Candlewick Press
Date: 2007
ISBN #: 0763615781
Genre: Historical Fiction
Synopsis: A collection of short one-person plays featuring characters, between ten and fifteen years old, who live in or near a thirteenth-century English manor.
Audience: Young Adult
Award: Newbery Medal Winner 2008
Curricular Connections:
Topics: Drama and Theater, Europe, Medieval, Plays and Skits
Discussion Questions and Journal Prompts:
What did you learn about medieval times from this story?
Have you read a story similar to this one? How was it the same or different?
What made the characters in this story believable?
Activities for Differentiated Instruction:
Act out one of the plays for your classmates.
Create a diorama with a scene from the book.
Make a wanted poster for one of the characters in the book.

Title: *Gym Candy*
Author: Carl Deuker
Author Web Site: http://members.authorsguild.net/carldeuker/
Publisher: Houghton Mifflin
Date: 2007
ISBN #: 0547076312
Genre: Fiction
Synopsis: Groomed by his father to be a star player, football is the only thing that has ever really mattered to Mick Johnson, who works hard for a spot on the varsity team his freshman year, then tries to hold onto his edge by using steroids, despite the consequences to his health and social life.
Audience: Young Adult
Curricular Connections
Topics: Family Life, Fathers and Sons, Football, High School, Steroids
Discussion Questions and Journal Prompts:
Was the actual game of football an important part of the story? Explain.
What do you know about the problem of steroids and sports?
Did the main character in the story change? If so, how?
Activities for Differentiated Instruction:
Create a newspaper article about this book for the sports column.
Create a crossword puzzle using ten football terms.
Research your favorite college or professional football player and write a description.

Title: *Hush: An Irish Princess Tale*
Author: Donna Jo Napoli
Author Web Site: http://www.donnajonapoli.com
Publisher: Atheneum Books for Young Readers
Date: 2007
ISBN #: 0689861796
Genre: Fiction
Synopsis: Fifteen-year-old Melkorka, an Irish princess, is kidnapped by Russian slave traders and learns not only how to survive but to challenge some of the brutality of her captors, who are fascinated by her apparent muteness and the possibility that she is enchanted.
Audience: Young Adult
Curricular Connections
Topics: Ireland, Middle Ages, Seafaring Life, Selective Mutism, Slavery
Discussion Questions and Journal Prompts:
What lesson(s) did you learn from this story?
Did you find the story difficult or easy to read? Why?
If you were the author would you have changed the story in any way? If so, how?
Activities for Differentiated Instruction:
Research Russian slave traders. Were they active in Ireland? Make a chart of facts.
Write an epilogue to the story.
Draw/create an ad for a teen magazine about the story.

Title: *Impossible*
Author: Nancy Werlin
Author Web Site: http://www.nancywerlin.com
Publisher: Dial Books
Date: 2008
ISBN #: 0803730020
Genre: Fiction
Synopsis: When seventeen-year-old Lucy discovers her family is under an ancient curse by an evil elfin knight, she realizes that to break the curse, she must perform three impossible tasks before her daughter is born to save them both.
Audience: Young Adult
Curricular Connections
Topics: Elves, Magic, Pregnancy, Teenage Mothers
Discussion Questions and Journal Prompts:
What was the turning point in the story?
Were the characters believable? What about the elfin knight?
Is the setting important to the story? How?
Activities for Differentiated Instruction:
Write an outline for turning this story into a play.
Create a bulletin board about magic and curses.
Create an oral book review, tape it, and play it for the class.

From *Differentiating Reading Instructing Using Children's Literature* by Liz Knowles, Ed.D.
Santa Barbara, CA: Libraries Unlimited. Copyright © 2009.

Title: *Little Brother*
Author: Cory Doctorow
Author Web Site: http://www.craphead.com
Publisher: Tor Teen
Date: 2008
ISBN #: 0765319853
Genre: Fiction
Synopsis: After being interrogated for days by the Department of Homeland Security in the aftermath of a major terrorist attack on San Francisco, California, seventeen-year-old Marcus, released into what is now a police state, decides to use his expertise in computer hacking to set things right.
Audience: Young Adult
Curricular Connections
Topics: Civil Rights, Computer Hackers, Counterculture, Department of Homeland Security, Terrorism
Discussion Questions and Journal Prompts:
If there were a sequel to this story, what would happen?
What did you learn about human nature from reading this book?
What qualities of the main character do you find admirable?
Activities for Differentiated Instruction:
Create a TV news report about the terrorist attack that occurred in this book.
Research the Department of Homeland Security and create a fact sheet about it.
Make a timeline of events from the story.

Title: *Love, Stargirl*
Author: Jerry Spinelli
Author Web Site: http://www.jerryspinelli.com
Publisher: Alfred A. Knopf/Borzoi
Date: 2007
ISBN #: 0375813756
Genre: Realistic Fiction
Synopsis: Still moping months after being dumped by her Arizona boyfriend Leo, fifteen-year-old Stargirl, a homeschooled free spirit, writes "the world's longest letter" to Leo, describing her new life in Pennsylvania.
Audience: Young Adult
Curricular Connections
Topics: Diaries, Eccentrics, Home Schooling, Pennsylvania
Discussion Questions and Journal Prompts:
Describe, in detail, the world's longest letter.
What do you like and dislike about this description of homeschooling?
What was it about Pennsylvania that you found interesting?
Activities for Differentiated Instruction:
Create a travel brochure for Pennsylvania.
Draw a picture of Stargirl.
Write a poem about Stargirl.

Title: *Me, the Missing and the Dead*
Author: Jenny Valentine
Author Web Site: http://www.jennyvalentine.com
Publisher: HarperTeen
Date: 2008
ISBN #: 006085068X
Genre: Fiction
Synopsis: When a series of chance events leaves him in possession of an urn with ashes, sixteen-year-old Londoner Lucas Swain becomes convinced that its occupant, Violet Park, is communicating with him, initiating a voyage of self-discovery that forces him finally to confront the events surrounding his father's sudden disappearance.
Audience: Young Adult
Curricular Connections
Topics: Fathers, London, England, Missing Persons, Single-Parent Families
Discussion Questions and Journal Prompts:
What were the surprises in this book?
When you selected this book, what did you think the story would be about? Were you right or wrong?
What was the mood of the story?
Activities for Differentiated Instruction:
Create a character chart of the main character, describing his traits and characteristics.
Write a letter to the main character, giving him advice about his part in the story.
Draw a promotional bookmark for the book.

Title: *November Blues*
Author: Sharon M. Draper
Author Web Site: http://sharondraper.com/
Publisher: Atheneum
Date: 2007
ISBN #: 1416906983
Genre: Realistic Fiction
Synopsis: A teenaged boy's death in a hazing accident has lasting effects on his pregnant girlfriend and his guilt-ridden cousin, who gives up a promising music career to play football during his senior year in high school.
Audience: Young Adult
Award: Coretta Scott King Author Honor Book 2008
Curricular Connections:
Topics: African Americans, High School, Teenage Pregnancy
Discussion Questions and Journal Prompts:
Was there enough or too much description in the story? Explain.
What made you angry or sad about the story?
What was stronger, the plot or the characters?
Activities for Differentiated Instruction:
Look at the author's Web site and create a poster about her and her books.
Write a *New York Times*–style book review of the book.
Create an award for a character and explain why he or she won the award.

From *Differentiating Reading Instructing Using Children's Literature* by Liz Knowles, Ed.D.
Santa Barbara, CA: Libraries Unlimited. Copyright © 2009.

Title: *One Whole and Perfect Day*
Author: Judith Clarke
Author Web Site: http://biography.jrank.org/pages/1849/Clarke-Judith-1943.html
Publisher: Front Street
Date: 2007
ISBN #: 1932425950
Genre: Fiction
Synopsis: As her irritating family prepares to celebrate her grandfather's eightieth birthday, sixteen-year-old Lily yearns for just one whole perfect day together.
Audience: Young Adult
Award: Michael L. Printz Award Honor Book 2008
Curricular Connections
Topics: Friendship, Intergenerational Relationships
Discussion Questions and Journal Prompts:
Do you agree or disagree with the feelings of the main character? Explain.
Did the story setting influence the story? How?
If you were the author of the story, would you have changed it? How?
Activities for Differentiated Instruction:
Rewrite the last chapter.
Create a Venn diagram comparing yourself to the main character.
Create a greeting card to send to the main character.

Title: *Repossessed*
Author: A. M. Jenkins
Author Web Site: http://www.harpercollins.com/authors/15325/A_M_Jenkins/index.aspx
Publisher: HarperTeen
Date: 2007
ISBN #: 0060835682
Genre: Fiction
Synopsis: A fallen angel, tired of being unappreciated while doing his pointless, demeaning boy's job, leaves Hell, enters the body of a seventeen-year-old boy, and tries to experience the full range of human feelings before being caught and punished, while his family and friends puzzle over the boy's changed behavior.
Audience: Young Adult
Award: Michael L. Printz Award Honor Book 2008
Curricular Connections
Topics: High School, Interpersonal Relations, Spirit Possessions
Discussion Questions and Journal Prompts:
What was the lesson or moral of the story?
What was the turning point in the story?
Why did you select this book? Did it meet your expectations?
Activities for Differentiated Instruction:
Write an epilogue.
Videotape a commercial for the book.
Illustrate an important event in the story and write a brief description.

Title: *Rights of the Accused*
Author: Michelle Lewis (editor)
Publisher: Thompson Gale/Greenhaven Press
Date: 2007
ISBN #: 0737727951
Genre: Nonfiction
Synopsis: This book covers the presumption of innocence, the right to counsel, the right to a trial by jury, and the right to confront one's accusers.
Audience: Young Adult
Curricular Connections
Topics: Criminal Procedure, Due Process of Law
Discussion Questions and Journal Prompts:
Was the book easy or difficult to understand? Explain.
Describe due process. Did the book help you to understand what it is?
Is it important that you know about this topic? Why or why not?
Activities for Differentiated Instruction:
Read an important or informative passage from the book for your classmates.
Make a poster for this book.
Write three further questions you have that are still unanswered after reading this book.

Title: *Rucker Park Setup*
Author: Paul Volponi
Author Web Site: http://www.paulvolponibooks.com
Publisher: Viking Press
Date: 2007
ISBN #: 0142412074
Genre: Fiction
Synopsis: While playing in a crucial basketball game on the very court where his best friend was murdered, Mackey tries to come to terms with his own part in that murder and decide whether to maintain his silence or tell J.R.'s father and the police what really happened.
Audience: Young Adult
Curricular Connections
Topics: African Americans, Basketball, Best Friends, Harlem, Murder
Discussion Questions and Journal Prompts:
What did you learn from the main character in this story?
Would this book make a good movie? Why or why not?
Has the story changed the way you think about telling the truth? Explain.
Activities for Differentiated Instruction:
Create a teen magazine ad for the story.
Retell the story in a four-frame cartoon.
Review the story for a newspaper column called "Teen Reads."

From *Differentiating Reading Instructing Using Children's Literature* by Liz Knowles, Ed.D.
Santa Barbara, CA: Libraries Unlimited. Copyright © 2009.

Title: *Stress 101: An Overview for Teens*
Author: Margaret O. Hyde and Elizabeth H. Forsyth
Publisher: Twenty-First Century Books
Date: 2008
ISBN #: 0822567881
Genre: Nonfiction
Synopsis: This book provides information about what stress does to your body and your brain, your heart, immune system, and gut. It tells how to gain control and outwit stress through meditation and provides other tools for reducing stress.
Audience: Young Adult
Curricular Connections
Topics: Stress Management, Teens and Stress
Discussion Questions and Journal Prompts:
Does the format of the book help to clarify the information? Why or why not?
What were the three most important things you learned from the book?
Did the book change the way you think about stress? Explain.
Activities for Differentiated Instruction:
Create a poster with key information about stress for display in your classroom.
Write a ten-word crossword puzzle highlighting information from the book.
Make a collage about stress using pictures from a magazine.

Title: *Superbugs Strike Back*
Author: Connie Goldsmith
Publisher: Twenty-First Century Books
Date: 2007
ISBN #: 0822566079
Genre: Nonfiction
Synopsis: This book tells about bacterial basics, the search for cures, and antibiotics versus bacteria, and describes the superbugs.
Audience: Young Adult
Curricular Connections
Topics: Antibiotics, Drug Resistance in Microorganisms
Discussion Questions and Journal Prompts:
What did you learn from this book?
What further questions do you have after reading this book? Write at least three.
What are the consequences to the problems described in this book?
Activities for Differentiated Instruction:
Make a labeled drawing of a superbug.
Make an acrostic using terms from the book.
Write an investigative piece about superbugs for a science column in a newspaper.

Title: *The Boxer and the Spy*
Author: Robert B. Parker
Author Web Site: http://www.robertbparker.net
Publisher: Philomel Books
Date: 2008
ISBN #: 0399247750
Genre: Fiction
Synopsis: Fifteen-year-old Terry, an aspiring boxer, uncovers the mystery behind the unexpected death of a classmate.
Audience: Young Adult
Curricular Connections
Topics: Boxing, Mystery and Detective Stories
Discussion Questions and Journal Prompts:
What made this book a good mystery story?
The author usually writes general fiction for adults. Was the story easy to read and follow? Explain.
What did you like and dislike about the main character?
Activities for Differentiated Instruction:
Create a poster about the author.
Rewrite the ending of the story.
Change the title of the story. Give several choices.

Title: *The Boy Who Dared*
Author: Susan Campbell Bartoletti
Author Web Site: http://www.scbartoletti.com
Publisher: Scholastic Press
Date: 2008
ISBN #: 0439680131
Genre: Historical Fiction
Synopsis: In October 1942, seventeen-year-old Helmuth Hübener, imprisoned for distributing anti-Nazi leaflets, recalls his past life and how he came to dedicate himself to the truth about Hitler and the war to the German people.
Audience: Young Adult
Curricular Connections
Topics: Anti-Nazi Movement, Courage, Germany—History, Helmuth Hübener (1925–1942)
Discussion Questions and Journal Prompts:
Has the story changed the way you think?
What characteristics did Hübener have?
Why did the author think this topic was important?
Activities for Differentiated Instruction:
Research the life of Hübener and write a report to share with your classmates.
Go to the author's web site and create a poster about her and her books.
Write a letter about the book to Hübener.

From *Differentiating Reading Instructing Using Children's Literature* by Liz Knowles, Ed.D. Santa Barbara, CA: Libraries Unlimited. Copyright © 2009.

Title: *The House of Djinn*
Author: Suzanne Fisher Staples
Author Web Site: http://www.suzannefisherstaples.com
Publisher: Farrar, Straus & Giroux/Frances Foster Books
Date: 2008
ISBN #: 0374399360
Genre: Fiction
Synopsis: An unexpected death brings Shabanu's daughter, Mumtaz, and nephew, Jameel, both aged fifteen, to the forefront of an attempt to modernize Pakistan, but the teens must both sacrifice their own dreams if they are to meet family and tribal expectations.
Audience: Young Adult
Curricular Connections
Topics: Family Life, Pakistan, Spirits
Discussion Questions and Journal Prompts:
What did you learn from this story?
What did you learn about Pakistan from this story?
What difficult decisions do the two main characters face?
Activities for Differentiated Instruction:
Make a poster with a map and facts about Pakistan.
Write an epilogue for this story.
Make a list of the good and the not-so-good parts of the book.

Title: *The Last Girls of Pompeii*
Author: Kathryn Lasky
Author Web Site: http://www.kathrynlasky.com
Publisher: Viking
Date: 2007
ISBN #: 0670061964
Genre: Fiction
Synopsis: Twelve-year-old Julia knows her physical deformity will keep her from normal life, but she counts on the continuing friendship of her lifelong slave, Mitka, until they learn that both their futures in first-century Pompeii are about to change for the worse.
Audience: Young Adult
Curricular Connections
Topics: Family Life, People with Disabilities, Pompeii, Rome, Slavery, Vesuvius, Volcanic Eruptions
Discussion Questions and Journal Prompts:
What happened that changed the lives of Julia and Mitka?
What was it like to be a slave in Ancient Rome? How were slaves treated?
What did you learn about friendship from this story?
Activities for Differentiated Instruction:
Create a travel brochure for Ancient Rome.
Research Vesuvius and write a report about it.
Create a bookmark about the author.

Title: *Triangle Shirtwaist Factory Fire*
Author: Donna Getzinger
Author Web Site: http://www.authorsden.com/visit/author.asp?AuthorID=652
Publisher: Morgan Reynolds
Date: 2008
ISBN #: 1599350998
Genre: Nonfiction
Synopsis: This book describes industry, immigration, and the makings of a tragedy on March 25, 1911. Those who perished in the aftermath of the inferno did not die in vain. However, the dilemma of sweatshops has outlived the fire.
Audience: Young Adult
Curricular Connections
Topics: Clothing Factories, Fires—New York, Labor Laws and Legislation, Sweatshops, Triangle Shirtwaist Company
Discussion Questions and Journal Prompts:
How could this tragedy have been prevented?
What did you learn from reading this book?
Why did the author think this topic was important?
Activities for Differentiated Instruction:
Write a letter to the author with your comments about the book.
Videotape a TV news report describing the fire.
Use several different sources to write a report about sweatshops.

Title: *Trouble*
Author: Gary D. Schmidt
Author Web Site: http://www.houghtonmifflinbooks.com/catalog/authordetail.cfm?authorID=2696
Publisher: Clarion Books
Date: 2008
ISBN #: 0618927662
Genre: Fiction
Synopsis: Fourteen-year-old Henry, wishing to honor his brother Franklin's dying wish, sets out to hike Maine's Mount Katahdin with his best friend and dog. But fate adds another companion—the Cambodian refugee accused of fatally injuring Franklin—and reveals troubles that predate the accident.
Audience: Young Adult
Curricular Connections
Topics: Cambodian Americans, Death, Dogs, Refugees, Traffic Accidents
Discussion Questions and Journal Prompts:
What surprising thing did you learn in this story?
What kind of person is Henry? Describe his character traits.
Tell what you liked and disliked about the ending of the story.
Activities for Differentiated Instruction:
Create a travel brochure for Maine and include Mount Katahdin.
Research the author and create a poster about him and his other books.
Write a letter to a friend telling why you recommend this book.

From *Differentiating Reading Instructing Using Children's Literature* by Liz Knowles, Ed.D.
Santa Barbara, CA: Libraries Unlimited. Copyright © 2009.

Title: *Unwind*
Author: Neal Shusterman
Author Web Site: http://www.storyman.com
Publisher: Simon & Schuster Books for Young Readers
Date: 2007
ISBN #: 1416912045
Genre: Science Fiction
Synopsis: In a future world where those between the ages of thirteen and eighteen can have their lives "unwound" and their body parts harvested for use by others, three teens go to extreme lengths to uphold their beliefs—and perhaps save their own lives.
Audience: Young Adult
Curricular Connections
Topics: Fugitives from Justice, Revolutionaries, Survival Skills
Discussion Questions and Journal Prompts:
Was the ending satisfactory and why, or how would you have changed it?
What makes this an unusual survival story?
What characteristics do the three teens demonstrate in the story?
Activities for Differentiated Instruction:
Create an auto license plate for a character in the book.
Write a five-entry diary for one of the girls in the book.
Draw a picture of the setting of this story.

Title: *Waiting for Normal*
Author: Leslie Connor
Author Web Site: http://www.harpercollins.com/authors/30604/Leslie_Connor/index.aspx
Publisher: HarperCollins/Katherine Tegen Books
Date: 2008
ISBN #: 0060890886
Genre: Fiction
Synopsis: Twelve-year-old Addie tries to cope with her mother's erratic behavior and being separated from her beloved stepfather and half-sisters when she and her mother go to live in a small trailer by the railroad tracks on the outskirts of Schenectady, New York.
Audience: Young Adult
Curricular Connections
Topics: Family Problems, Mothers, Self-reliance, Stepfathers
Discussion Questions and Journal Prompts:
What did you learn about family problems from this book?
What kind of a person is Addie?
Was the setting of this story important to the outcome?
Activities for Differentiated Instruction:
Write a letter about this book to the author.
Create an acrostic about self-reliance with words from this book.
Write a *New York Times*–style book review for this book.

Title: *War in the Middle East: A Reporter's Story*
Author: Wilborn Hampton
Author Web Site: http://www.answers.com/topic/wilborn-hampton
Publisher: Candlewick Press
Date: 2007
ISBN #: 0763624934
Genre: Nonfiction
Synopsis: A documentary containing the author's experiences covering two pivotal wars and offering readers a portrait of major world events.
Audience: Young Adult
Curricular Connections
Topics: Middle East, Military
Discussion Questions and Journal Prompts:
What solutions, if any, does the author offer?
Does this book help you to better understand the conflict? Explain.
Are you able to draw implications for the future from the information in this book? Explain.
Activities for Differentiated Instruction:
Write a letter about the book to a classmate.
Create a timeline of events that are described in the book.
Create a map showing the locations described in this book.

Title: *Wednesday Wars*
Author: Gary D. Schmidt
Author Web Site: http://www.goodreads.com/author/show/96375.Gary_D_Schmidt
Publisher: Clarion Books
Date: 2007
ISBN #: 0618724834
Genre: Historical Fiction
Synopsis: During the 1967 school year, on Wednesday afternoons when all his classmates go either to Catechism or Hebrew school, seventh-grader Holling Hoodhood stays in Mrs. Baker's classroom where they read the plays of William Shakespeare. Holling learns much of value about the world he lives in.
Audience: Young Adult
Award: Newbery Medal Honor Book 2008
Curricular Connections:
Topics: 1960s, School, Vietnam War
Discussion Questions and Journal Prompts:
What did you find to be unusual about this story?
What was the most interesting idea you got from the story?
If you were the author, would you change the ending? Why or why not?
Activities for Differentiated Instruction:
Write a newspaper article about William Shakespeare.
Adapt this story into a play.
Create a bulletin board about this book.

From *Differentiating Reading Instructing Using Children's Literature* by Liz Knowles, Ed.D.
Santa Barbara, CA: Libraries Unlimited. Copyright © 2009.

Title: *White Darkness*
Author: Geraldine McCaughrean
Author Web Site: http://www.geraldinemccaughrean.com
Publisher: HarperTeen
Date: 2007
ISBN #: 0060890355
Genre: Fiction
Synopsis: Taken to Antarctica by the man she thinks of as her uncle for what she believes to be a vacation, Symone—a troubled fourteen year old—discovers that he is dangerously obsessed with seeking Symme's Hole, an opening that supposedly leads into the center of a hollow Earth.
Audience: Young Adult
Award: Michael L. Printz Award Winner 2008
Curricular Connections
Topics: Antarctica, Explorations, Polar Regions, Survival
Discussion Questions and Journal Prompts:
What did you learn about Antarctica from this book?
What was the mood of the story? Did it change?
What would you ask the author about this book?
Activities for Differentiated Instruction:
Research Antarctica; is there really a place called Symme's Hole? If so, tell about it.
Make a ten-word crossword for this book.
Write your own story, making it very different but with the same title as this book.

Title: *Yellow Flag*
Author: Robert Lipsyte
Author Web Site: http://www.robertlipsyte.com
Publisher: HarperCollins/HarperTeen
Date: 2007
ISBN #: 0060557079
Genre: Fiction
Synopsis: When seventeen-year-old Kyle reluctantly succumbs to family pressure and replaces his injured brother in the family race car, he struggles to keep up with his trumpet playing while deciding how—or if—he can continue making music with a brass quintet and headlines as a NASCAR racer.
Audience: Young Adult
Curricular Connections
Topics: Self-actualization, Auto Racing, Family, North Carolina, Trumpet
Discussion Questions and Journal Prompts:
What is your opinion of Kyle trying to race and also play the trumpet?
What expectations does your family have for you?
What kind of person is Kyle? Describe all his character traits.
Activities for Differentiated Instruction:
Create a collage about cars and racing.
Write a newspaper sports column about Kyle's NASCAR racing.
Create a bumper sticker for the book.

Title: *Your Own, Sylvia: A Verse Portrait of Sylvia Plath*
Author: Stephanie Hemphill
Publisher: Knopf Books for Young Readers
Date: 2007
ISBN #: 0375837999
Genre: Fiction
Synopsis: The author interprets the people, events, influences, and art that made up the brief life of Sylvia Plath.
Audience: Young Adult
Award: Michael L. Printz Award Honor Book 2008
Curricular Connections
Topics: Mental Illness, Poetry, Writer
Discussion Questions and Journal Prompts:
What did you learn from this book?
Describe the presentation of Plath's life in the book. Was it effective? Explain.
How did the information in the story change the way you think?
Activities for Differentiated Instruction:
Share information about Sylvia Plath with your classmates.
Create a double acrostic from the book.
Draw a picture of the saddest part of the book and write a brief description.

From *Differentiating Reading Instructing Using Children's Literature* by Liz Knowles, Ed.D.
Santa Barbara, CA: Libraries Unlimited. Copyright © 2009.

Author Information

Adler, David
Birthplace: New York, New York
Date of Birth: April 10, 1947
Current Home: Woodmere, New York
Interesting Information:
David was very artistic growing up. As he got older, he drew cartoons and sold a few.
David worked as a math teacher for nine years.
He's a dreamer and said that dreamers become writers.
Web Site: http://www.davidaadler.com
Contact: camj563@aol.com

Almond, David
Birthplace: Newcastle, England
Date of Birth: May 15, 1951
Current Home: Northumberland, England
Interesting Information:
He always wanted to be a writer.
He sold his house and lived in a commune so he could concentrate on his writing.
His favorite subject in school was cookery.
Web Site: http://www.davidalmond.com
Contact: http://hodderheadline.co.uk

Auch, Mary Jane
Birthplace: Mineola, New York
Current Home: Rochester, New York
Interesting Information:
She wrote plays and put them on in her garage and sold tickets.
She designed prints for men's pajamas at one point.
She just loves chickens.
Web Site: http://www.mjauch.com
Contact: mjauch@rochester.rr.com

Avi (Michael Avi-Yonah)
Birthplace: Brooklyn, New York
Date of Birth: December 27, 1937
Current Home: Providence, Rhode Island
Interesting Information:
Got the nickname Avi from his sister.
He has a learning disability that makes writing by hand difficult.
Avi says the key to good writing is reading.
Web Site: http://www.avi-writer.com

107

Contact:
  c/o HarperCollins
  1350 Avenue of the Americas
  New York, NY 10019

Bartoletti, Susan Campbell
Birthplace: Harrisburg, Pennsylvania
Date of Birth: November 18, 1958
Current Home: near Scranton, Pennsylvania
Interesting Information:
  Her dad died in a car accident when she was a child.
  She took horseback riding lessons, piano lessons, and art lessons growing up.
  As a child, she had dogs, cats, hamsters, guinea pigs, ducks, parakeets, and a goat.
Web Site: http://www.scbartoletti.com
Contact: susan@scbartoletti.com

Bauer, Marion Dane
Birthplace: Oglesby, Illinois
Date of Birth: November 20, 1938
Current Home: Eden Prairie, Minnesota
Interesting Information:
  She was the editor of her yearbook.
  She always filled her home with foster kids and exchange students as well as her own two children.
  She started kindergarten early at the age of four.
Web Site: http://www.mariondanebauer.com
Contact: mdb@mariondanebauer.com

Berenstain, Jan
Birthplace: Philadelphia, Pennsylvania
Date of Birth: July 26, 1926
Current Home: Bucks County, Pennsylvania
Interesting Information:
  During World War II, she did engineering drawing for the military.
  She loves the theater.
  She once wrote a cartoon series.
Web Site: http:// www.berenstainbears.com
Contact:
  c/o HarperCollins Children's Books
  1350 Avenue of the Americas
  New York, NY 10019

Brett, Jan
Birthplace: Massachusetts
Date of Birth: December 1, 1949
Current Home: seacoast town in Massachusetts
Interesting Information:
  As a child, she spent many hours reading and drawing.

She has a hedgehog as a pet named Buffy.

She loves to travel for inspiration.

Web Site: http://www.janbrett.com

Contact: http://www.janbrett.com/emailjb.html

Bruchac, Joseph

Birthplace: Saratoga Springs, New York

Date of Birth: October 19, 1942

Current Home: Greenfield Center, New York

Interesting Information:

Raised by his grandparents, he was an avid reader from childhood.

He plays guitar, flute, and drum—he sometimes plays songs he writes.

Bruchac says we must learn to listen to each other and to the earth.

Web Site: http://www.josephbruchac.com

Contact:

P.O. Box 308

Greenfield Center, NY 12833

Phone: (518) 584-1728

Fax: (518) 583-9741

E-mail: nudatlog@earthlink.net

Bunting, Eve

Birthplace: December 12, 1928

Date of Birth: Maghera, Northern Ireland

Current Home: Pasadena, California

Interesting Information:

Her greatest joy is writing picture books.

Her dad used to read poetry to her on rainy days in front of the fire.

Her mom started the first lending library in her town.

Web Site: http://www.kidsreads.com/authors/au-bunting-eve.asp

Contact:

c/o Clarion Books

215 Park Avenue South

New York, NY 10003

Carlson, Nancy

Birthplace: Edina, Minnesota

Date of Birth: October 10, 1953

Current Home: Bloomington, Minnesota

Interesting Information:

In kindergarten, she said she wanted to "make pictures and tell stories."

She likes running, hiking, biking, swimming, skiing, and bird watching.

She has two kids, a guinea pig, and a dog named Lily.

Web Site: http://www.nancycarlson.com

Contact: info@nancycarlson.com

Christelow, Eileen
Birthplace: Washington, DC
Date of Birth: April 22, 1943
Current Home: Vermont
Interesting Information:
>She did not have a TV until she was twelve.
>She was only allowed to watch the TV for an hour and a half every week.
>She earned a living as a photographer and graphic designer while writing.

Web Site: http://www.christelow.com
Contact: See link in author's Web site.

Clements, Andrew
Birthplace: Camden, New Jersey
Date of Birth: May 29, 1949
Current Home: Westborough, Massachusetts
Interesting Information:
>He played guitar and wrote songs.
>He writes in a shed in his backyard, with a woodstove and an air-conditioning unit.
>He has four sons.

Web Site: http://www.andrewclements.com
Contact:
>c/o Simon & Schuster
>1230 Avenue of the Americas
>New York, NY 10020

Coville, Bruce
Birthplace: Syracuse, New York
Date of Birth: May 16, 1950
Current Home: Syracuse, New York
Interesting Information:
>He has wanted to be a writer since sixth grade.
>He has written musical plays, contributed to anthologies of fantasy stories, and written picture books.
>He is fascinated by myths and mythical imagery.

Web Site: http://www.brucecoville.com/
Contact:
>Oddly Enough
>PO Box 6110
>Syracuse, NY 13217

Creech, Sharon
Birthplace: South Euclid, Ohio
Date of Birth: July 29, 1945
Current Home: Pennington, New Jersey
Interesting Information:
>She has one sister and three brothers. She says she had a noisy and rowdy family.
>*Walk Two Moons* is based on her five-day car trip to Idaho, when she was 12 years old.
>She wanted to be a painter, ice-skater, singer, teacher, or a reporter.

Web Site: http://www.sharoncreech.com/
Contact:
 c/o HarperCollins Children's Books
 Author Mail
 1350 Avenue of the Americas
 New York, NY 10019

Crutcher, Chris
Birthplace: Dayton, Ohio
Date of Birth: July 17, 1946
Current Home: Spokane, Washington
Interesting Information:
 He did not like to read as a child.
 He was an excellent swimmer and runner.
 He became a child and family therapist.
Web Site: http://www.aboutcrutcher.com/
Contact: Stotan717@aol.com

Curtis, Christopher Paul
Birthplace: Flint, Michigan
Date of Birth: May 10, 1953
Current Home: Windsor, Ontario, Canada
Interesting Information:
 He spent his first 13 years after high school on an assembly line of Flint's Historic Fisher Body plant, hanging car doors on Buicks.
 Both of his grandfathers were entertainers, one being Earl "Lefty" Lewis, a baseball league pitcher, and the other Herman Curtis Sr., a bandleader.
 The characters in his book *Bud, Not Buddy* are modeled after his grandfathers.
Web Site: http://www.randomhouse.com/features/christopherpaulcurtis/
Contact: http://www.cpc.cogeco.ca

Cushman, Karen
Birthplace: Chicago, Illinois
Date of Birth: October 4, 1941
Current Home: Vashon Island west of Seattle, Washington
Interesting Information:
 When she was younger, she wanted to be a librarian, a movie star, or a tap dancer.
 She remembers reading anything she could get her hands on when she was growing up: comic books, Russian novels, books about World War II, *Mad Magazine*, and cereal boxes.
 She makes her home with her husband Philip, a cat and a dog, and lots of books, flowers, and tomato plants.
Web Site: http://www.ipl.org.div/askauthor/chusmanbio.html
Contact:
 c/o HarperCollins Children's Books
 Author Mail
 1350 Avenue of the Americas
 New York, NY 10019

dePaola, Tomie
Birthplace: Meriden, Connecticut
Date of Birth: September 15, 1934
Current Home: New London, New Hampshire
Interesting Information:
> He has written and illustrated over 200 books.
> His favorite color is white, and he loves popcorn and Christmas.
> He lives in a 200-year-old renovated barn.

Web Site: http://www.tomie.com
Contact:
> c/o Penguin Young Readers Group
> 345 Hudson Street
> New York, NY 10014

Deuker, Carl
Birthplace: San Francisco, California
Date of Birth: August 26, 1950
Current Home: Seattle, Washington
Interesting Information:
> He writes books about good kids who sometimes do foolish things.
> He is a teacher and writes before and sometimes after work.
> He has a pet guinea pig.

Web Site: http://members.authorsguild.net/carldeuker/bio.htm
Contact: carl1989@hotmail.com

DiCamillo, Kate
Birthplace: Philadelphia, Pennsylvania
Date of Birth: March 25, 1964
Current Home: Minneapolis, Minnesota
Interesting Information:
> She is short and loud.
> She hates to cook and loves to eat.
> She is single and childless, but has lots of friends and is an aunt to three lovely children (Luke, Roxanne, and Max) and one not so lovely dog (Henry).

Web Site: http://www.katedicamillo.com/
Contact:
> c/o Candlewick Press
> 99 Dover Street
> Somerville, MA 02144

Farmer, Nancy
Birthplace: Phoenix, Arizona
Date of Birth: July 19, 1941
Current Home: Menlo Park, California
Interesting Information:
> She worked the front desk of a hotel at nine years of age.
> She was in the Peace Corps.
> She was a chemistry teacher and an insect pathology technician.

Web Site: http://www.answers.com/topic/nancy-farmer-children-s-author
Contact:
 c/o Orchard Books
 95 Madison Avenue
 New York, NY 10016

Fleming, Denise
Birthplace: Toledo, Ohio
Date of Birth: January 31, 1950
Current Home: Toledo, Ohio
Interesting Information:
 She loves cats and has many.
 She loves stories about pioneers.
 She likes to paint, draw, papier-mâché, and do wood working.
Web Site: http://www.denisefleming.com
Contact: See link on the author's Web site.

Fox, Mem
Birthplace: Melbourne, Australia
Date of Birth: March, 1946
Current Home: Adelaide, Australia
Interesting Information:
 She grew up in Africa because her parents were missionaries.
 Her first book was rejected nine times.
 Literacy is her greatest passion.
Web Site: http://www.memfox.net
Contact: jda@jd-associates.com.au

Frasier, Debra
Birthplace: Vero Beach, Florida
Date of Birth: April 3, 1953
Current Home: Minneapolis, Minnesota
Interesting Information:
 She once constructed a costume puppet, 60 feet long, that took eight people to make it move.
 She always carries a small journal for her thoughts.
 For her fiftieth birthday, she purchased a canoe and is going to navigate fifty rivers and/or streams.
Web Site: http://www.debrafrasier.com
Contact: debrafrasier@mac.com

Freedman, Russell
Birthplace: San Francisco, California
Date of Birth: October 11, 1929
Current Home: New York, New York
Interesting Information:
 His father was a publishing rep for Macmillan, so famous authors often came to dinner at his house.
 His favorite books as a child were *Treasure Island* and *Wild Animals I Have Known*.
 His interest in wild animals continued into nonfiction in general.

Web Site: http://www2.scholastic.com/browse/contributor.jsp?id=1766
Contact:
    c/o Clarion Books
    215 Park Avenue South
    New York, NY 10003

Gantos, Jack

Birthplace: Mt. Pleasant, Pennsylvania
Date of Birth: July 2, 1951
Current Home: Boston, Massachusetts
Interesting Information:
    He has been writing since he was in sixth grade.
    His stories are based on his life—he really did have a cat exactly like Rotten Ralph!
    Hole in My Life is his prison memoir—he actually did time in prison.
Web Site: http://www.jackgantos.com
Contact:
    c/o Children's Marketing Department
    Farrar, Straus & Giroux Books for Young Readers
    19 Union Square West
    New York, NY 10003

George, Jean Craighead

Birthplace: Washington, DC
Date of Birth: July 2, 1919
Current Home: Chappaqua, New York
Interesting Information:
    Her first pet was a turkey vulture.
    She went to the Naval Arctic Research Lab in Alaska to learn how to talk to wolves.
    She began writing in the third grade.
Web Site: http://www.jeancraigheadgeorge.com
Contact: jeangeorge1@verizon.net

Giff, Patricia Reilly

Birthplace: Brooklyn, New York
Date of Birth: April 26, 1935
Current Home: Weston, Connecticut
Interesting Information:
    "I always start each day by writing, that's like breathing for me."
    Her favorite books growing up were, *Little Women, The Secret Garden,* Black Stallion books, Sue Barton books, and the Nancy Drew series.
    She enjoys reading in the bathtub, going to the movies, and eating popcorn.
Web Site: http://www.randomhouse.com/features/patriciareillygiff/
Contact:
    c/o Random House
    1540 Broadway
    New York, NY 10036

Grimes, Nikki
Birthplace: Harlem, New York
Date of Birth: October 20, 1950
Current Home: Corona, California
Interesting Information:
     She grew up in foster homes.
     She sang at the Stockholm Philharmonic in Sweden.
     She makes and sells her own line of jewelry and textiles.
Web Site: http://www.nikkigrimes.com
Contact:
     c/o Curtis Brown, Ltd.
     Ten Astor Place
     New York, NY 10003

Haddix, Margaret Peterson
Birthplace: Washington Court House, Ohio
Date of Birth: April 9, 1964
Current Home: Columbus, Ohio
Interesting Information:
     She had a short attention span during most all of her childhood.
     She spent much of her time reading and writing in secret.
     Her ideas came from past experiences.
Web Site: http://www.haddixbooks.com/
Contact:
     c/o Simon & Schuster Books for Young Readers
     1230 Avenue of the Americas
     New York, NY 10020

Henkes, Kevin
Birthplace: Racine, Wisconsin
Date of Birth: November 27, 1960
Current Home: Madison, Wisconsin
Interesting Information:
     He was a published author/illustrator at the age of 19.
     He thought he would be an artist until his junior year in high school.
     He never thought he'd be lucky enough to be a real author and illustrator.
Web Site: http://www.kevinhenkes.com
Contact:
     c/o GreenWillow Books
     1350 Avenue of the Americas
     New York, NY 10019

Hesse, Karen
Birthplace: Baltimore, Maryland
Date of Birth: August 29, 1952
Current Home: Brattleboro, Vermont

Interesting Information:

She wanted to be an archaeologist, an ambassador, an actor, or an author.

She attended Towson State College as a theater major.

A few of her past jobs were waitress, nanny, librarian, typesetter, and proofreader.

Web Site: http://www.kidsread.com/author/au-heese-karen.asp

Contact:

c/o Hyperion Books For Children

114 5th Avenue

New York, NY 10011

Hiassen, Carl

Birthplace: Plantation, Florida

Date of Birth: March 12, 1953

Current Home: Florida Keys

Interesting Information:

At age 23, he joined the *Miami Herald* as a general assignment reporter.

Since 1985, he has written a regular column in the Sunday *Herald*'s opinion/editorial section.

He got a typewriter when he was six and wrote a neighborhood sports paper and handed out carbon copies to his neighbors.

Web Site: http://www.carlhiaasen.com/

Contact: tgagnon@thelavinagency.com

Hinton, S. E. (Susan Eloise)

Birthplace: Tulsa, Oklahoma

Date of Birth: July 22, 1948

Current Home: Tulsa, Oklahoma

Interesting Information:

As a child, she was a tomboy who loved horses.

She read everything—all the time.

Royalties from *The Outsiders* helped her finance her education at the University of Tulsa.

Web Site: http://www.sehinton.com

Contact: sehinton@sehinton.com

Hobbs, Will

Birthplace: Pittsburgh, Pennsylvania

Date of Birth: August 22, 1947

Current Home: Durango, Colorado

Interesting Information:

Will was a reading teacher for many years before becoming a writer.

Will liked everything to do with the out-of-doors.

Ideas for his books come from his own experiences.

Web Site: http://www.willhobbsauthor.com

Contact:

5 Sunridge Circle

Durango, CO 81301

Holt, Kimberly Willis
Birthplace: Pensacola, Florida
Date of Birth: September 9, 1960
Current Home: Amarillo, Texas
Interesting Information:
  Her earliest memory is eating an orange dreamsicle at two years old.
  Her favorite color is green and favorite foods are dark chocolate, chicken and dumplings, and sushi.
  She moved around a lot as a child.
Web Site: http://www.kimberlywillisholt.com
Contact:
  PO Box 20135
  Amarillo, TX 79114

Howe, James
Birthplace: Oneida, New York
Date of Birth: August 2, 1946
Current Home: Hastings-on-the-Hudson, New York
Interesting Information:
  He loves animals.
  He wanted to be a jockey because he loves horses so much.
  His favorite book is *Charlotte's Web.*
Web Site: http://www2.scholastic.com/browse/collateral.jsp?id=1297_type=Contributor_typeId=3599
Contact:
  c/o Hyperion Books for Children
  114 Fifth Avenue
  New York, NY 10011

Hutchins, Pat
Birthplace: Yorkshire, England
Date of Birth: June 18, 1942
Current Home: Hampstead, England
Interesting Information:
  She recently received her honorary doctorate degree from Suffolk College.
  Her favorite color is yellow.
  She loves gardening, reading, and music.
Web Site: http://www.titch.net
Contact:
  Hutchins Film Company Ltd.
  PO Box 38207
  London, NW31ZE

Jacques, Brian
Birthplace: Liverpool, England
Date of Birth: June 15, 1939
Current Home: Liverpool, England
Interesting Information:
  His name is pronounced "jakes."

He started out as a seaman and traveled to many wonderful places.

He has been a fireman, a policeman, a truck driver, a bus driver, a boxer, and a comedian.

Web Site: http://www.redwall.org/

Contact:

Redwall Readers Club
P.O. Box 57
Mossley Hill
Liverpool, UK
L18 3NZ

Kimmel, Eric

Birthplace: Brooklyn, New York

Date of Birth: October 30, 1946

Current Home: Portland, Oregon

Interesting Information:

He worked in the U.S. Virgin Islands as a teacher and librarian.

He loves bluegrass music and plays the banjo.

He has one dog, two cats, and a large tank with tropical fish.

Web Site: http://www.ericakimmel.com

Contact: Kimmel@comcast.net

Korman, Gordon

Birthplace: Montreal, Quebec, Canada

Date of Birth: October 23, 1963

Current Home: Toronto, New York, Florida

Interesting Information:

He writes out his stories first in longhand and then types them into the computer.

Fifty percent of what he writes really happened—the rest is imaginary.

He travels over 40,000 miles a year to promote his books and talk to kids.

Web Site: http://gordonkorman.com/

Contact:

c/o Scholastic Inc.
555 Broadway
New York, NY 10012

Leedy, Loreen

Birthplace: Wilmington, Delaware

Date of Birth: June 15, 1959

Current Home: Central Florida

Interesting Information:

She used to make animal jewelry and chess sets out of polymer clay.

Her animal jewelry became the characters in her books.

She now makes jewelry out of beads and enjoys hiking, reading, and gardening.

Web Site: http://www.loreenleedy.com

Contact: LJLart@bellsouth.net

Lester, Julius
Birthplace: St. Louis, Missouri
Date of Birth: January 27, 1939
Current Home: Amherst, Massachusetts
Interesting Information:
He was politically active in the early Civil Rights movement in the South—three of his great-grandparents were slaves.
He became a musician and recorded two albums.
He was not a good writer in his younger years.
Web Site: http://members.authorsguild.net/juliuslester/
Contact: lester@judnea.umass.edu
306 Old Springfield Road
Belchertown, MA 01007-9694

Lowry, Lois
Birthplace: Honolulu, Hawaii
Date of Birth: March 20, 1937
Current Home: Massachusetts and Maine
Interesting Information:
She was a solitary child who lived in a world of books and her own vivid imagination.
Her dad was an army dentist, and she lived in Hawaii, New York, Pennsylvania, Tokyo, Rhode Island, and Washington, D.C.
She was married at the age of 19 and had four children in four and a half years.
Web Site: http://www.loislowry.com/
Contact: info@loislowry.com

Lubar, David
Birthplace: Morristown, New Jersey
Date of Birth: March 1955
Current Home: Pennsylvania
Interesting Information:
He loves to write about weird and fantastic creatures.
As a child and young adult, he loved to read—mostly science fiction.
He has written many computer games for Nintendo and GameBoy.
Web Site: http://www.davidlubar.com
Contact: david@davidlubar.com

Lynch, Chris
Birthplace: Boston, Massachusetts
Date of Birth: July 2, 1962
Current Home: Ayrshire, Scotland
Interesting Information:
He writes honestly about things that interest teens and tries to make each novel new and different.
His books are often controversial.
He has Irish citizenship and lives in Scotland.
He has three brothers and three sisters. He loves anything funny and he loves to laugh.
Web Site: http://www.harperchildrens.com/authorintro/index.asp?authorid=12419

Contact:
   c/o HarperCollins
   1350 Avenue of the Americas
   New York, NY 10019

Macaulay, David
Birthplace: England
Date of Birth: December 2, 1946
Current Home: Rhode Island
Interesting Information:
   He works in a studio a distance away from his home.
   At age 11, he moved with his family from England to New Jersey.
   He graduated from Rhode Island School of Design (RISD) and worked as an interior designer, a junior high school teacher, and a teacher at RISD.
Web Site: http://www.houghtonmifflinbooks.com/authors/macaulay/
Contact:
   146 Water Street
   Warren, RI 02885

MacLachlan, Patricia
Birthplace: Cheyenne, Wyoming
Date of Birth: March 3, 1938
Current Home: Williamsburg, Massachusetts
Interesting Information:
   She carries a little bag of prairie dirt to link her to her past.
   She used to love any book about dogs.
   She cowrites with her daughter.
Web Site: http://www.bookwire.com/MeetTheAuthor/Interview_Patricia_MacLachlan.htm
Contact:
   c/o Author Mail
   HarperCollins
   10 E. 53rd St.
   New York, NY 10022

McCully, Emily Arnold
Birthplace: Galesburg, Illinois
Date of Birth: July 1, 1939
Current Home: Chatham, New York
Interesting Information:
   She was a daredevil as a child and still is as an adult.
   She is an avid reader, gardener, cook, and tennis player.
   She is an actress and historian as well as an author.
Web Site: http://www.balkinbuddies.com/mccully/

McKissack, Patricia
Birthplace: Smyrna, Tennessee
Date of Birth: August 9, 1944
Current Home: St. Louis, Missouri
Interesting Information:
  She had pen pals in three different countries growing up.
  She taught for nine years and was an editor for six years.
  She loves to travel.
Web Site: http://voices.cla.umn.edu/vg/Bios/entries/mckissack_patricia.html
Contact:
  c/o All Writing Services
  225 S. Meramec # 206
  Clayton, MO 63115

McPhail, David
Birthplace: Newburyport, Massachusetts
Date of Birth: June 30, 1940
Current Home: Newburyport, Massachusetts
Interesting Information:
  He loved playing in the woods and making bows and arrows and tree houses.
  He's loved to draw since he was two.
  After he heard Elvis, he bought a guitar, took lessons, and joined a band that toured across America.
Web Site: http://www.friend.ly.net/users/jorban/biographies/mcphaildavid/index.htm
Contact:
  88 Lime Street
  Newburyport, MA 01950

Meddaugh, Susan
Birthplace: Montclair, New Jersey
Date of Birth: October 4, 1944
Current Home: Sherborn, Massachusetts
Interesting Information:
  She once worked as a book designer.
  She has a dog that was a stray and is named Martha.
  Her seven-year-old son gave her the idea about the first Martha book as he was eating alphabet soup
  and asked if the dog would talk if she ate it, too.
Web Site: http://www.patriciamnewman.com/meddaugh.html
Contact:
  56 Maple Street
  Sherborn, MA 01770

Myers, Walter Dean
Birthplace: Martinsburg, West Virginia
Date of Birth: August 12, 1937
Current Home: Jersey City, New Jersey
Interesting Information:
  His mother died when he was three, and his father gave him up for adoption.

His adopted parents lived in Harlem, where he grew up.

As a child, he had a speech impediment.

Web Site: http://www.walterdeanmyersbooks.com

Contact:

    c/o HarperCollins

    1350 Avenue of the Americas

    New York, NY 10019

Napoli, Donna Jo

Birthplace: Miami, Florida

Date of Birth: February 28, 1948

Current Home: Swarthmore, Pennsylvania

Interesting Information:

    She loves to garden and to bake.

    She has an interest in frogs and would love to live as a naturalist.

    She takes modern dance and yoga classes.

Web Site: http://www.donnajonapoli.com/

Contact: dnapoli1@swarthmore.edu

Nix, Garth

Birthplace: Melbourne, Australia

Date of Birth: July 19, 1963

Current Home: Sydney, Australia

Interesting Information:

    Garth has traveled to many strange places around the world.

    He spent five years as a part-time military man but did not like it.

    He likes to find new, young authors and help them get published.

Web Site: http://www.garthnix.co.uk/

Contact: garthnix@ozemail.com.au

Numeroff, Laura Joffe

Birthplace: Brooklyn, New York

Date of Birth: July 14, 1953

Current Home: Brentwood, California

Interesting Information:

    She was a Brownie and a Girl Scout.

    She loves to travel; she has been to every state except Montana, Idaho, Alaska, and Hawaii.

    She loves cats, dogs, horses, raccoons, otters, koala bears, llamas, and chimps.

Web Site: http://www.lauranumeroff.com/

Contact: email@lauranumeroff.com

O'Malley, Kevin

Date of Birth: 1961

Current Home: Baltimore, Maryland

Interesting Information:

    He was often sent to the library as a child for a time out.

    His favorite book growing up was *Where the Wild Things Are.*

He is often compared to the comedian Robin Williams.
Web Site: http://www.booksbyomalley.com/
Contact: komalley@comcast.net

Osborne, Mary Pope
Birthplace: Fort Sill, Oklahoma
Date of Birth: May 20, 1949
Current Home: Northwestern Connecticut
Interesting Information:
    Her father was in the military so she moved a lot as a child.
    She was a religion major in college.
    She once lived in a cave in Crete.
Web Site: http://www.marypopeosborne.com/
Contact:
    c/o Random House, Inc.
    1745 Broadway
    New York, NY 10019

Park, Linda Sue
Birthplace: Urbana, Illinois
Date of Birth: March 25, 1960
Current Home: Rochester, New York
Interesting Information:
    She started writing poems and stories when she was four years old.
    She had a haiku published when she was nine and was paid a dollar, which she framed and gave to her Dad. She still has it.
    She enjoys cooking, traveling, watching movies, doing the *New York Times* crossword puzzles, baseball, soccer, and board games.
Web Site: http://www.lspark.com/
Contact:
    c/o Clarion Books
    215 Park Avenue South
    New York, NY 10003

Paulsen, Gary
Birthplace: Minneapolis, Minnesota
Date of Birth: May 17, 1939
Current Home: New Mexico
Interesting Information:
    He ran away from home at 14 to tour with a traveling carnival.
    Three of his books are Newbery Honor books.
    He loves to interact with his fans.
Web Site: http://www.garypaulsen.com
Contact:
    c/o Children's Publicity
    1540 Broadway
    New York, NY 10036

Philbrick, Rodman
Birthplace: Boston, Massachusetts
Date of Birth: 1951
Current Home: Maine and Florida Keys
Interesting Information:
He started writing in sixth grade, but it was not "cool," so he became a "secret writer."
Once he stopped trying to write literary works and began telling stories, his books finally sold.
He says he has a kid's voice in his head that tells him what to write.
Web Site: http://www.rodmanphilbrick.com/
Contact:
P.O. Box 4149
Portsmouth, NH 03802-4149

Pinkwater, Daniel Manus
Birthplace: Memphis, Tennessee
Date of Birth: November 15, 1941
Current Home: Hoboken, New Jersey
Interesting Information:
He got into trouble in school because he used to pass funny notes in class to make his friends laugh out loud.
He won a short-story contest and won a subscription to *National Geographic* as a boy.
He is a commentator for National Public Radio.
Web Site: http://www.pinkwater.com/
Contact: See link on the author's Web site.

Polacco, Patricia
Birthplace: Lansing, Michigan
Date of Birth: July 11, 1944
Current Home: Union City, Michigan
Interesting Information:
A meteor fell in her front yard when she was a child.
She did not learn to read till she was fourteen because she has dyslexia.
She did not have a TV growing up.
Web Site: http://www.patriciapolacco.com/
Contact: babushka.inc@verizon.net

Prelutsky, Jack
Birthplace: Bronx, New York
Date of Birth: September 8, 1940
Current Home: Seattle, Washington
Interesting Information:
He took piano and voice lessons growing up.
He was once a cab driver.
He now enjoys photography and carpentry.
Web Site: http://www.jackprelutsky.com/
Contact:
c/o Greenwillow Books

1350 Avenue of the Americas
New York, NY 10019

Pullman, Philip
Birthplace: Norwich, England
Date of Birth: October 19, 1946
Current Home: Oxford, England
Interesting Information:
As a child, he loved reading comic books, especially Superman and Batman.
He has received the highest award given for children's literature in England.
He writes in a shed in the garden behind his home in England.
Web Site: http://www.philip-pullman.com
Contact: feedback@philip-pullman.com

Raschka, Chris
Birthplace: Huntington, Pennsylvania
Date of Birth: March 6, 1959
Current Home: New York, New York
Interesting Information:
He worked in a home for handicapped children in St. Croix for eight years.
He is a master player of the viola.
His hobbies are knitting and surfing.
Web Site: http://www.kidspoint.org/columns2.asp?column_id=1318&column_type=author
Contact:
310 Riverside Drive # 418
New York, NY 10025

Rodman, Mary Ann
Birthplace: Washington, DC
Date of Birth: March 26
Current Home: Alpharetta, Georgia
Interesting Information:
She likes to collect music CDs.
She always writes with music on.
She taught herself to read at age three.
Web Site: http://www.maryannrodman.com/
Contact: maryannrodman@maryannrodman.com

Rowling, J. K.
Birthplace: Chipping Sudbury, England
Date of Birth: July 31, 1965
Current Home: Edinburgh, Scotland
Interesting Information:
Before she sold her first book, she was on welfare.
She always wanted to be a writer.
Some of the names in her books are made up, and some are real.
Web Site: http://www.jkrowling.com

Contact:
   c/o Scholastic, Inc.
   555 Broadway
   New York, NY 10012

Rubel, Nicole
Birthplace: Coral Gables, Florida
Date of Birth: April 29, 1953
Current Home: Aurora, Oregon
Interesting Information:
   She has an identical twin sister.
   She has a cat, a dog, horses, and sheep.
   A significant theme in her stories is finding oneself and learning to express one's feelings and thoughts.
Web Site: http://www.nicolerubel.com/
Contact: Nicole@nicolerubel.com

Ryan, Pam Muñoz
Birthplace: Bakersfield, California
Date of Birth: December 25, 1951
Current Home: North San Diego County, California
Interesting Information:
   She is the oldest of three sisters and the oldest of 23 cousins.
   She is Spanish, Mexican, Basque, Italian, and Oklahoman.
   She spent her summers riding her bike to the library.
Web Site: http://www.pammunozryan.com/
Contact: PMunozRyan@aol.com
   c/o Scholastic, Inc.
   557 Broadway
   New York, NY 10012-3999

Rylant, Cynthia
Birthplace: Hopewell, Virginia
Date of Birth: June 6, 1954
Current Home: Eugene, Oregon
Interesting Information:
   She grew up with her mother and her grandparents.
   She grew up very poor with no car, no electricity, and no running water.
   She worked as a waitress and a librarian.
Web Site: http://falcon.jmu.edu/~ramseyil/rylant.htm

Sachar, Louis
Birthplace: East Meadow, New York
Date of Birth: March 20, 1954
Current Home: Austin, Texas
   He especially liked math in school but began to love reading in high school.
   During college, he worked as a teacher's helper and was known as Louis the Yard Teacher, because he always supervised the kids at lunch recess.

He went to law school and passed the bar exam, but decided he wanted to write books.
Web Site: http://louissachar.com/
Contact:
> c/o Farrar, Straus & Giroux
> 19 Union Square West
> New York, NY 10003

Salisbury, Graham
Birthplace: Philadelphia, Pennsylvania
Date of Birth: April 11, 1944
Current Home: Portland, Oregon
Interesting Information:
> He did not read as a child.
> He flunked English twice in college.
> Now he loves to read and encourages everyone who wants to write to read, read, read.

Web Site: http://www.grahamsalisbury.com
Contact: graham@grahamsalisbury.com

Scieszka, Jon
Birthplace: Flint, Michigan
Date of Birth: September 8, 1954
Current Home: Brooklyn, New York
Interesting Information:
> He was a first- and second-grade teacher and studied writing at Columbia University.
> He likes dark humor, but his audience is hardcore silly kids.
> Someone said he makes the book equivalent of a happy meal.

Web Site: http://www.guysread.com
Contact:
> c/o Children's Marketing
> Penguin USA
> 345 Hudson Street
> New York, NY 10014

Selznick, Brian
Birthplace: East Brunswick, New Jersey
Date of Birth: July 14, 1966
Current Home: Brooklyn, New York, and San Diego, California
Interesting Information:
> He used to paint windows for holidays at the bookstore he worked for.
> He wants to be a set designer.
> He loves monster movies.

Web Site: http://www.theinventionofhugocabret.com/index.htm
Contact:
> c/o Random House/Alfred A. Knopf Books for Young Readers
> 201 E. 50th Street
> New York, NY 10022

Shan, Darren (O'Shaughnessy)
Birthplace: London, England
Date of Birth: July 2, 1972
Current Home: Limerick, Ireland
Interesting Information:
> His real name is Darren O'Shaughnessy and he lives in Limerick, England.
> He began writing at age 14 and finished his first novel at 17.
> He mostly writes for adults; *Cirque De Freak* was his first book for children.
> He made a seven-figure deal with Warner Brothers for the movie rights to the first two Cirque books.

Web Site: http://www.darrenshan.com
Contact:
> c/o Paul Kenny
> Rahina
> Clarina
> County Limerick, Ireland

Shannon, David
Birthplace: Washington, D.C.
Date of Birth: October 5, 1960
Current Home: Los Angeles, California
Interesting Information:
> He is a passionate baseball fan and softball player.
> He first drew the pictures for *No, David!* when he was five years old.
> He likes to read history books and biographies.

Web Site: http://www.answers.com/topic/david-shannon-childrens-author

Shusterman, Neal
Birthplace: New York, New York
Date of Birth: November 12, 1962
Current Home: Dove Canyon, California
Interesting Information:
> *Charlie & the Chocolate Factory* and the movie *Jaws* influenced his decision to become a writer.
> As a summer camp counselor, he became known as the storyteller.
> Books played an important part in his life as he was growing up.

Web Site: http://www.storyman.com/
Contact: nstoryman@aol.com
> PO Box 18516
> Irvine, CA 95623-8516

Sis, Peter
Birthplace: Brno, Czechoslovakia
Date of Birth: May 11, 1949
Current Home: New York City area
Interesting Information:
> Peter was in the United States making a film for his government and decided to stay and was granted asylum.
> His is also an acclaimed artist.
> His film work is in the permanent collection of the Museum of Modern Art, New York.

Web Site: http://www.petersis.com/index2.html
Contact:
    c/o Children's Marketing Department
    Farrar, Strauss & Giroux/Books for Young Readers
    19 Union Square West
    New York, NY 10003

Sleator, William
Birthplace: Harve de Grace, Maryland
Date of Birth: February 13, 1945
Current Home: Boston, Massachusetts
Interesting Information:
    He was the rehearsal pianist for the Boston Ballet Company before he started writing.
    He is considered to be the country's most original science fiction writer for teens.
    He has a second home in Thailand.
Web Site: http://www.tycho.org./sleator.shtml
Contact: wsleator1@aol.com
    77 Worcester Street
    Boston, MA 02118

Snicket, Lemony (Daniel Handler)
Birthplace: San Francisco, California
Date of Birth: February 28, 1970
Current Home: Sacramento, California
Interesting Information:
    Handler graduated from Wesleyan University in 1992.
    He is an alumnus of the San Francisco Boys Chorus.
    Handler is married to Lisa Brown, a graphic artist he met in college; they have a son, Otto, who was born in 2003.
Web Site: http://www.lemonysnicket.com
Contact:
    c/o HarperCollins
    1350 Avenue of the Americas
    New York, NY 10019

Soto, Gary
Birthplace: Fresno, California
Date of Birth: April 19, 1952
Current Home: Berkeley, California
Interesting Information:
    He was a factory laborer.
    He grew up in poverty.
    His dad died in an accident when he was five.
Web Site: http://www.garysoto.com/
Contact:
    43 The Crescent
    Berkeley, CA 94708

Spinelli, Eileen
Birthplace: South Philadelphia, Pennsylvania
Date of Birth: August 16, 1942
Current Home: West Chester, Pennsylvania
Interesting Information:
    Her first desk to write on was made of orange crates.
    She loves the changing of the seasons.
    She has six children and 16 grandchildren.
Web Site: http://www.eileenspinelli.com/heart_001.htm
Contact: Eileen@eileenspinelli.com

Spinelli, Jerry
Birthplace: Norristown, Pennsylvania
Date of Birth: February 1, 1941
Current Home: Phoenixville, Pennsylvania
Interesting Information:
    As a child he wanted to become a major league shortstop.
    He first tried to write for adults but was unsuccessful.
    He married a woman with six children and started writing for kids.
Web Site: http://www.jerryspinelli.com
Contact: jerry@jerryspinelli.com

Stanley, Diane
Birthplace: Abilene, Texas
Date of Birth: December 27, 1943
Current Home: Santa Fe, New Mexico
Interesting Information:
    She was a medical illustrator.
    Her hobbies are traveling, skiing, hiking, and gardening.
    She travels to the actual locations for the settings of her books to be accurate.
Web Site: http://www.dianestanley.com/
Contact: dianley@aol.com

Stein, David Ezra
Birthplace: Brooklyn, New York
Current Home: Kew Gardens, New York
Interesting Information:
    He studied theater and illustration in college.
    He is a set illustrator as well as an author.
    He loves to daydream and doodle.
Web Site: http://www.davidezra.com/
Contact: david@davidezra.com

Stevens, Janet
Birthplace: Dallas, Texas
Date of Birth: January 17, 1953
Current Home: Colorado

Interesting Information:
    She moved around a lot as a child because her father was in the military.
    Her favorite color is periwinkle blue.
    She loves to draw the rhinoceros because of all the wrinkles.
Web Site: http://www.janetstevens.com/
Contact: rhinoink@aol.com

Strasser, Todd
Birthplace: New York, New York
Date of Birth: May 5, 1950
Current Home: Larchmont, New York
Interesting Information:
    He has published more than 100 books, and in three years, he wrote and published 24 books.
    He is very concerned about school violence and how readily available guns are.
    He is currently writing a book on homeless street kids.
Web Site: http://www.toddstrasser.com
Contact:
    c/o Scholastic, Inc.
    555 Broadway
    New York, NY 10012

Tang, Greg
Birthplace: Ithaca, New York
Current Home: Massachusetts
Interesting Information:
    He loves to play hockey and tennis.
    He got the idea to write a math book by looking at dominoes.
    His father taught electrical engineering at Cornell University, and his mother taught mathematics at Ithaca College.
Web Site: http://www.gregtang.com/
Contact: gregtang@gregtang.com

Taylor, Theodore
Birthplace: Statesville, North Carolina
Date of Birth: June 23, 1921
Current Home: Laguna Beach, California
Interesting Information:
    He thinks of himself as a reporter.
    He joined the Merchant Marines at age 21.
    He writes seven days a week except during football season, when he takes the weekends off.
Web Site: http://www.theodoretaylor.com
Contact:
    c/o Publicity Dept.
    Bantam Doubleday Dell
    1540 Broadway
    New York, NY 10036

Thaler, Mike
Birthplace: Los Angeles, California
Date of Birth: October 8, 1936
Current Home: Canby, Oregon
Interesting Information:
> He used to draw cartoons for adults.
> His home is on a Christmas tree farm.
> His favorite color is yellow.

Web Site: http://www.mikethaler.com/
Contact: mike@mikethaler.com

Thompson, Lauren
Birthplace: Oregon
Date of Birth: 1962
Current Home: Brooklyn, New York
Interesting Information:
> She lived in the Netherlands for two years and spoke Dutch.
> She likes to ride her bike and play baseball.
> The ideas that matter to her are ones that remind her of something special in her childhood.

Web Site: http://www.laurenthompson.net/
Contact:
> c/o Simon & Schuster Books for Young Readers
> 1230 Avenue of the Americas
> New York, NY 10020

Van Allsburg, Chris
Birthplace: Grand Rapids, Michigan
Date of Birth: June 18, 1949
Current Home: Providence, Rhone Island
Interesting Information:
> He majored in sculpture in college and is a professional artist. He has had many gallery shows.
> He likes to bike ride and play tennis.
> His family used to run a creamery.

Web Site: http://www.chrisvanallsburg.com/about.html
Contact: info@chrisvanallsburg.com

Viorst, Judith
Birthplace: Newark, New Jersey
Date of Birth: February 2, 1931
Current Home: Washington, D.C.
Interesting Information:
> She studied Freudian psychology.
> She is a psychoanalysis researcher as well as an author.
> She is an Emmy-winning poet.

Web Site: http://www.kennedy-center.org/programs/family/alexander/author.html

Contact:
    c/o Robert Lescher—Lescher & Lescher
    67 Irving Place
    New York, NY 10003

Wells, Rosemary
Birthplace: New York, New York
Date of Birth: January 23, 1943
Current Home: Westchester County, New York
Interesting Information:
    Max and Ruby are based on her daughters' experiences.
    She would love to work for the FBI.
    She writes and/or draws for eight hours a day.
Web Site: http://www.rosemarywells.com/
Contact: See the link on the author's Web site.

Wheeler, Lisa
Birthplace: Pennsylvania
Date of Birth: 1963
Current Home: Detroit, Michigan
Interesting Information:
    Her favorite color is yellow, even though it's hard on the eyes.
    She was very shy as a child and spent her lunch hours in the library.
    She collects Mother Goose books.
Web Site: http://www.lisawheelerbooks.com/
Contact: lawheel2@comcast.net

Wiesner, David
Birthplace: Bridgewater, New Jersey
Date of Birth: February 5, 1956
Current Home: Philadelphia
Interesting Information:
    Growing up, he wrote comic books on a drafting table that his father gave him.
    Most of the objects from his books come from the wallpaper in the bedroom where David grew up.
    He was very shy growing up.
Web Site: http://www.houghtonmifflinbooks.com/authors/wiesner/home.html
Contact:
    c/o Dilys Evans
    PO Box 400
    Norfolk, CT 06058

Willems, Mo
Birthplace: New Orleans, Louisiana
Date of Birth: February 11, 1968
Current Home: Massachusetts
Interesting Information:
    He won six Emmy awards for his writing on *Sesame Street.*

His illustrations, wire sculpture, and carved ceramics have been exhibited in galleries and museums across the nation.

After graduating from college, Mo traveled Europe for a year and drew a cartoon every day. They are all published in a book.

Web Site: http://www.mowillems.com/

Contact:

    c/o Christian Trimmer

    Hyperion Books for Children

    114 5th Avenue, 15th Floor

    New York, NY 10011

Wilson, Karma

Birthplace: North Idaho

Current Home: Montana

Interesting Information:

    She only got three channels on her home TV growing up.

    Her hobbies are reading, baking, and photography.

    She started writing after she bought her first computer and learned how to type.

Web Site: http://www.bearsnoreson.com/

Contact: See the link on the author's Web site.

Wood, Audrey

Birthplace: Little Rock, Arkansas

Date of Birth: 1948

Current Home: Santa Barbara, California

Interesting Information:

    She could swim before she could walk.

    She learned to walk at seven months old.

    She grew up around circus performers because her dad helped paint murals for them.

Web Site: http://www.audreywood.com/

Contact:

    c/o Simon and Schuster

    1230 Avenue of the Americas

    New York, NY 10020

Woodson, Jacqueline

Birthplace: Columbus, Ohio

Date of Birth: February 12, 1963

Current Home: Brooklyn, New York

Interesting Information:

    In fifth grade, she edited her school's literary magazine.

    She does not believe in censorship.

    She writes about things that actually happen to kids that adults don't want to talk about.

Web Site: http://www.jacquelinewoodson.com

Contact:

    c/o Bantam Doubleday Dell

    1540 Broadway

    New York, NY 10036

Wynne-Jones, Tim
Birthplace: Brombourough, Cheshire, Great Britain
Date of Birth: August 12, 1948
Current Home: Perth, Ontario, Canada
Interesting Information:
    He writes song lyrics.
    He is the lead singer in the band Louis the Dreamer.
    He lives on 76 acres in Canada.
Web Site: http://www.timwynne-jones.com/
Contact:
    Rural Route No. 4
    Perth, Ontario
    K7H 3C6, Canada

Yolen, Jane
Birthplace: New York, New York
Date of Birth: February 11, 1939
Current Home: Hatfield, Massachusetts
Interesting Information:
    Both of Jane's parents and her brothers are writers.
    She has published well over 250 books—she writes for all grade levels and in multiple genres.
    She calls herself an "Arthurholic."
Web Site: http://www.janeyolen.com
Contact: janeyolen@aol.com

Ziefert, Harriet
Birthplace: North Bergen, New Jersey
Date of Birth: July 7, 1941
Current Home: Maplewood, New Jersey, and Lincoln, Massachusetts
Interesting Information:
    She writes most of her books within twelve hours.
    She has taught every elementary grade from K–6.
    She had hoped to be an editor.
Web Site: http://biography.jrank.org/pages/977/Ziefert-Harriet-1941.html
Contact:
    Blue Apple Books
    515 South Valley St.
    Maplewood, NJ 07040

Annotated Resources

Allen, Janet. *Words, Words, Words: Teaching Vocabulary in Grades 4–12.* Stenhouse Publishers, 1999.
This is a wonderful tool for teaching vocabulary with topics that include a vocabulary-rich classroom, word control, using context, and alternatives to "look it up in the dictionary!"

Allington, Richard. *What Really Matters for Struggling Readers: Designing Research-Based Programs.* Longman, 2001.
Allington discusses reading instruction in American schools. What he believes really matters is that kids need to read a lot and books they can read fluently. They also need to develop thoughtful literacy, and teachers need to know how to provide appropriate instruction for struggling readers.

Allington, Richard. *What Really Matters in Fluency: Research-Based Practices across the Curriculum.* Pearson, 2009.
Allington discusses the meaning of fluency and why it is such a hot topic, how it is developed normally, how to assess it, and how to develop it in struggling readers.

Altwerger, Bess, Nancy Jordan, & Nancy Shelton. *Rereading Fluency: Process, Practice, and Policy.* Heinemann, 2007.
Richard Allington provides the foreward in this book about fluency. It provides a new look at fluency, the relationship between fluency and comprehension, and phonics versus literature programs. It discusses whether fluency can measure the difference between more and less proficient readers and whether it should be considered a critical component of reading.

Angelillo, Janet. *Writing about Reading—From Book Talk to Literary Essays, Grades 3–8.* Heinemann, 2003.
This resource discusses thinking and talking about texts, using a reader's notebook, various genres, the literary essay, writing and reading in the content areas, evaluating written work, and transforming students into lifelong readers.

Atwell, Nancie. *The Reading Zone: How to Help Kids Become Skilled, Passionate, Habitual, Critical Readers.* Scholastic, 2007.
Atwell, an author with a focus on middle school students, tells how to get students of this age to enjoy reading and to read successfully. Topics include in the zone, choice, comprehension, booktalking, boys and reading, and high school.

Brassell, Danny, & Timothy Rasinski. *Comprehension That Works: Taking Students beyond Ordinary Understanding to Deep Comprehension.* Shell Education, 2008.
Brassell and Rasinski discuss engaging student interest, what proficient readers do, identifying difficulties with comprehension, differentiating instruction, and comprehension strategies.

Carbo, Marie. *Becoming a Great Teacher of Reading: Achieving High Rapid Reading Gains with Powerful, Differentiated Strategies.* Corwin Press, 2007.
Carbo begins with the focus point that all students can learn. She suggests teaching to natural strengths and using a continuum of reading methods, the Carbo Reading Method, active learning, visual dyslexia, and preparing students for tests.

Chapman, Anne. *Making Sense: Critical Reading across the Curriculum.* The College Board, 1993.

> This book defines ten areas—here are eight: foster reading with understanding, encourage wide reading, use multicultural stories, talk to readers about their reading, observe how kids read, avoid nagging and criticizing, acknowledge that mistakes are OK, and help students make positive changes in their reading habits.

Chapman, Carolyn, & Rita King. *Differentiated Instructional Strategies for Reading in the Content Areas.* Corwin Press, 2003.

> The key to successful differentiation in the content areas is attention to the climate, knowing the reader, various reading models, vocabulary, and word analysis.

Cunningham, Patricia, & Richard Allington. *Classrooms That Work: They Can All Read and Write.* Addison-Wesley Longman, 1999.

> This book provides great strategies for teaching reading. It covers developing decoding and spelling fluency; strategies for reading in science and social studies; guiding children's reading and writing; actual lessons from kindergarten, primary, and intermediate classrooms; and reading beyond the classroom.

Daniels, Harvey, & Marilyn Bizar. *Teaching the Best Practice Way, Methods That Matter. K–12.* Stenhouse Publishers, 2005.

> Best practice resources are always important to review. This one includes reading as thinking, publishing and creating, small-group work, classroom workshops, authentic experiences, reflective assessment, and integrative units.

Fogarty, Robin. *Differentiated Learning: Different Strokes for Different Folks.* Fogarty & Associates, 2001.

> There are three elements in differentiated learning: change (content, process, product), challenge, and choice.

Fogarty, Robin. *Literacy Matters: Strategies Every Teacher Can Use.* Corwin Press, 2007.

> Fogarty provides a number of easy-to-use strategies for approaching literacy. The text includes learning to learn with metacognitive reflections, seven strategies for teaching comprehension, using prior knowledge to support schema theory, using brain and learning principles, reading attitude matters, intervention strategies, teaching vocabulary using technology, reading aloud, multiple intelligences, and guided reading.

Forsten, Char, Jim Grant, & Betty Hollas. *Differentiated Instruction: Different Strategies for Different Learners, Grades K–8.* Crystal Springs Books, 2002.

> Remembering that there is no one standard student profile, this book gives practical information about curriculum compacting, tiered activities, learning centers, flexible grouping, and mentoring.

Forsten, Char, Jim Grant, & Betty Hollas. *Differentiating Textbooks, Strategies to Improve Student Comprehension & Motivation.* Crystal Springs Books, 2003.

> Topics include ways to create random groupings, adapting textbooks, and before, during, and after reading strategies.

Furr, David. *Reading Clinic: A New Way to Teach Reading (Brain Research Applied to Reading).* Truman House, 2000.

> This book demonstrates a new method for teaching reading using brain research. It is called the neuro-reading method. The method includes perceptual, syntactic, and semantic processes; word

recognition; and comprehension. There are step-by-step lessons and appendices filled with helpful information.

Golon, Alexandra Shires. *Visual-Spatial Learners: Differentiation Strategies for Creating a Successful Classroom.* Prufrock Press, 2008.

This is an excellent resource for differentiation that includes discussion about learning styles, both visual and auditory, in reading; creative writing; writing by hand versus keyboarding; spelling; note taking; learning math facts; and organizational skills.

Gregory, Gayle, & Carolyn Chapman. *Differentiated Instructional Strategies: One Size Doesn't Fit All.* Corwin Press, 2002.

This book provides information on planning for differentiated instruction, levels of thinking, and learning styles.

Hinchman, Kathleen, & Heather Sheridan-Thomas (eds.). *Best Practices in Adolescent Literacy Instruction.* Guilford Press, 2008.

This resource includes nineteen essays from important researchers in the field of literacy. They are organized under three categories: perspectives toward adolescent literacy instruction, developing reading and writing strategies for multiple contexts, and adolescent literacy program issues.

Hollas, Betty. *Differentiating Instruction in a Whole-Group Setting: Taking Easy First Steps into Differentiation.* Crystal Springs Books, 2005.

There are four windows for differentiation: student engagement, questioning, flexible grouping, and ongoing assessment. This resource gives important information and practical activities for each.

Jacobs, Heidi Hayes. *Active Literacy across the Curriculum: Strategies for Reading, Writing, Speaking, and Listening.* Eye on Education, 2006.

Jacobs provides information for every teacher on becoming an active language teacher, teaching ESOL students, note taking, editing, revising, speaking, listening and revising, and integrating curriculum maps for grades K–12.

Jalongo, Mary. *Young Children and Picture Books.* National Association for the Education of Young Children, 2004.

This book focuses on the question, why read aloud to children who can read independently? According to Jalongo, there are seven reasons: to foster appreciation, extend background and interest, expand preferences, develop listening comprehension, model what good readers do, share literature responses, and entertain and encourage child development in language arts.

Jensen, Eric. *Teaching with the Brain in Mind.* Association for Supervision and Curriculum Development, 1998.

This is a practical guide to using brain research in the classroom. It covers all aspects of learning but includes some important messages about teaching reading. Jensen states that children should be read to starting at six months of age. Challenging vocabulary is best learned before twelve years of age. In most cases, it is better to teach sight words before phonics (whole before parts).

Johnson, Holly, & Lauren Freedman. *Content Area Literature Circles: Using Discussion for Learning across the Curriculum.* Christopher-Gordon Publishers, 2005.
>   A great resource for creating a climate of comfortable book discussion in the content area classrooms.

Knowles, Elizabeth, & Martha Smith. *Boys and Literacy: Practical Strategies for Librarians, Teachers, and Parents.* Libraries Unlimited, 2005.
>   Eleven topics are explored specifically for boys, and the text includes discussion questions, an annotated and a regular bibliography, and also author information and a list of magazines for boys.

Knowles, Elizabeth, & Martha Smith. *Reading Rules! Motivating Teens to Read.* Libraries Unlimited, 2001.
>   Filled with ideas, practical tips, useful statistics, and other helpful data on teen reading, this book details numerous methods for getting teens to read, such as reading workshops, literature circles, book clubs, and booktalks. An overview of YA literature and annotated bibliographies of both teen and professional reads further assists in creating a literacy plan.

Krashen, Stephen. *The Power of Reading: Insights from the Research.* Libraries Unlimited, 2004.
>   Emeritus professor of education at the University of Southern California, Krashen is the founder of free voluntary reading (FVR). This book covers FVR, direct instruction, benefits of reading, and reading and cognitive development.

Marzano, Robert, Debra Pickering, & Jane Pollack. *Classroom Instruction That Works: Research-Based Strategies for Increasing Student Achievement.* Association for Supervision and Curriculum Development, 2001.
>   Marzano and coauthors provide information on research-based strategies for teaching including similarities, differences, summarizing, note taking, homework, and generating and testing hypotheses, with specific applications for each.

McKenna, Michael. *Help for Struggling Readers: Strategies for Grades 3–8.* The Guilford Press, 2008.
>   Strategies include decoding, fluency, vocabulary, comprehension, and questioning.

McQuillan, J. *The Literacy Crisis: False Claims, Real Solutions.* Heinemann, 1998.
>   This book states that above all, it is necessary to provide good books for kids. There are seven important points with regard to the literacy crisis as it was seen in 1998. Children are reading as well, if not better, than 25 years ago; scores are fairly stable over the same time period; dyslexia is not as rampant as once thought; there have been slight increases in reading test results over the past 50 years; U.S. students are good readers on a worldwide scale; scores are fairly stationary; and whole language did not undermine reading scores in California.

Neuman, S., D. Celano, A. Greco, & P. Shue. *Access for All: Closing the Book Gap for Children in Early Education.* International Reading Association, 2001.
>   This resource highlights the importance of providing books for all children starting at a very early age. It includes a national survey of access to books at early childhood centers and provides suggestions for how to get books into the hands of those who need them most.

Nichols, Maria. *Talking about Text: Guiding Students to Increase Comprehension through Purposeful Talk.* Shell Education, 2008.
>   This resource provides information on the changing role of the classroom teacher, teaching purposeful talk behavior, and creating habits of mind that encourage students to read, think, and talk independently.

Opitz, M., & T. Rasinski. *Good-Bye Round Robin*. Heinemann, 1998.

This title provides information about the potentially harmful effects of round robin reading on students who are struggling readers. It provides many great suggestions for safe reading aloud with practice time beforehand.

Perez, Kathy. *More than 100 Brain-Friendly Tools and Strategies for Literacy Instruction*. Corwin Press, 2008.

This book is a wonderful resource for brain-friendly activities. It includes puzzles, strategies, classroom management tips, many examples of differentiation, and basic instructional strategies.

Reis, Sally M., & Joseph S. Renzulli. *Curriculum Compacting: An Easy Start to Differentiating for High-Potential Students*. Prufrock Press, 2005.

Everything you wanted to know about curriculum compacting, including its definition, how to use it, and how to implement it in the classroom.

Reutzel, D. R., & R. B. Cooter. *Teaching Children to Read: From Basals to Books*. Merrill, 1996.

This was one of my favorite texts for teaching reading to college students working on an elementary education degree. It describes three methods for teaching reading and states that no single one works; sometimes parts of all three are needed. The three methods are decoding, skills, and balanced. The skills method includes letters and sounds, sight words, and story structure. The balanced method includes whole language, read-alouds, independent reading, authentic writing, and themes.

Robb, Laura. *Differentiating Reading Instruction: How to Teach Reading to Meet the Needs of Each Student*. Scholastic, 2008.

This resource covers reaching all learners with best practice teaching; the foundations for differentiated reading instruction; whole-class, small-group, and independent reading instruction; and writing instruction.

Robb, Laura. *Teaching Reading in the Middle School: A Strategic Approach to Teaching Reading That Improves Comprehension and Thinking*. Scholastic, 2000.

This book lists some ways to support struggling readers in the middle school classroom. Teachers should be positive, set reasonable goals for students, get students actively involved in their learning, and try using different strategies when the usual ones aren't working. The teacher should be prepared to work one-on-one for extra explanations when other things aren't working. Students should be given extra time to process, they should be given opportunities to retell information in small groups, and it is important to make sure that the students understand all directions. Some struggling readers should have the help of a reading specialist, then they should regularly reflect on their progress.

Routman, Regie. *Reading Essentials: The Specifics You Need to Teach Reading Well*. Heinemann, 2003.

This is an excellent resource for all those interested in developing lifelong readers. It includes information on bonding with students, stressing that there is no one way or right way to teach reading, ideas for excellent teaching of reading, creating an excellent classroom library, building an independent reading program for all students, using reading programs as resources, and managing your time.

Sousa, David A. *How the Brain Learns to Read*. Corwin Press, 2005.

Sousa begins with a discussion of the process of learning spoken language and the various levels of language comprehension. Learning to read is not a natural ability, and Sousa discusses early stages of learning to read, comprehension, memory, and the importance of practice. Next he shares information about the teaching of reading, modern methods, and research findings. There are two chapters on recognizing and overcoming reading problems. There is also a section about the importance of content area reading and how important it is to make a good effort to close the reading achievement gap.

Sprenger, Marilee. *Becoming a "Wiz" at Brain-Based Teaching: How to Make Every Year Your Best Year.* Corwin Press, 2002.

Students need choices, and they need to have opportunities to work together and discuss outcomes. They need to journal about reading. They need challenging activities and lots of teacher feedback.

Sprenger, Marilee. *Differentiation through Learning Styles and Memory.* Corwin Press, 2008.

Sprenger talks about creating environments for learning, getting to know students' learning styles and how they remember, and differentiation for the visual and auditory and kinesthetic learner.

Tate, Marcia. *Worksheets Don't Grow Dendrites: 20 Instructional Strategies That Engage the Brain.* Corwin Press, 2003.

Some of the important strategies include questioning, discussion, drawing and illustrating, graphic organizers, mind maps, and webs for understanding, group discussion, drama, storytelling, writing, and journaling.

Tomlinson, Carol Ann. *The Differentiated Classroom: Responding to the Needs of All Learners.* Association for Supervision and Curriculum Development, 1999.

This book explains how you can meet the diverse needs of all the students in your classroom. Tomlinson describes the five key concepts: content, process, product, affect, and learning environment. Implementing differentiated instruction empowers students to learn through multiple and varied opportunities for practice.

Tomlinson, Carol Ann. *How to Differentiate Instruction in Mixed-Ability Classrooms.* Association for Supervision and Curriculum Development, 2001.

Tomlinson first clarifies what differentiated instruction is and isn't, then she discusses the rationale, role of the teacher, learning environment, strategies, how to plan interesting lessons, and how to differentiate content.

Tomlinson, Carol, & Jay McTighe. *Integrating Differentiated Instruction and Understanding by Design: Connecting Content and Kids.* Association for Supervision and Curriculum Development, 2006.

The authors draw a parallel between the two concepts, showing that they are very similar and noting the importance of knowing where you want to be by the end of a certain unit or skill set.

Tovani, Cris. *Do I Really Have to Teach Reading? Content Comprehension, Grades 6-12.* Stenhouse Publishers, 2004.

It has been proven that content area teachers must be reading teachers as well, and this reference provides strategies for all middle and high school teachers. Topics include comprehension, note taking, group work, and assessment.

Tyner, Beverly. *Small-Group Reading Instruction: A Differentiated Reading Model for Beginning and Struggling Readers.* International Reading Association, 2004.

This resource describes beginning reading instruction and small groups in the differentiated reading model, planning and assessing, instructional strategies, the different stages of reading (emergent, beginning, fledgling, transitional, and independent), early reading screening instruments, and word study.

Tyner, Beverly, & Sharon Green. *Small-Group Reading Instruction: A Differentiated Teaching Model for Intermediate Readers, Grades 3–8*. International Reading Association, 2005.

This resource describes instruction and small groups in the differentiated reading model, different stages of reading (evolving, maturing, advanced), assessment, and management.

Walpole, Sharon, & Michael McKenna. *Differentiated Reading Instruction: Strategies for the Primary Grades*. Guilford Press, 2007.

This resource focuses on differentiating reading instruction for the primary grades by using assessments, differentiating phonemic awareness instruction, and building word recognition, fluency, vocabulary, and comprehension. It provides lesson plans for kindergarten through third grades.

Welch, Rollie James. *The Guy-Friendly YA Library: Serving Male Teens*. Libraries Unlimited, 2007.

This is a wonderful resource for librarians and teachers of male teens. The topics include understanding teen males, their reading habits, books they like, providing library programs for them, booktalks, and a great list of popular titles for male teens.

Wolfe, Patricia, & Pamela Nevills. *Building the Reading Brain, PreK–3*. Corwin Press & Sage Publications, 2004.

Beginning with the nature of reading, this resource includes an informative section on what happens to the brain when children read, breaking the reading code, comprehension and vocabulary, and helping at-risk readers.

Wormeli, Rick. *Differentiation: From Planning to Practice Grades 6–12*. Stenhouse Publishers, 2007.

Wormeli begins with a frame of reference about differentiated instruction and includes a sample of a differentiated lesson; he next suggests helpful structures and strategies, then includes cognitive science structures and tips and finishes with 12 samples of differentiated learning experiences from multiple subjects.

Zemelman, Steven, Harvey Daniels, & Arthur Hyde. *Best Practice: New Standards for Teaching and Learning in America's Schools*. Heinemann, 1998.

This resource covers all school disciplines, but the section on best practices in teaching reading is especially important and timeless. It reviews an exemplary program, discusses the reading wars, lists the National Council of Teachers of English standards for language arts, and describes 14 best practices for teaching reading. It concludes with ways that parents and school principals can help.

Works Cited

Allington, Richard. *What Really Matters for Struggling Readers: Designing Research-Based Programs.* Longman, 2001.

Allington, Richard. *What Really Matters in Fluency: Research-Based Practices across the Curriculum.* Pearson, 2009.

Altwerger, Bess, Nancy Jordan, & Nancy Shelton. *Rereading Fluency: Process, Practice, and Policy.* Heinemann, 2007.

Angelillo, Janet. *Writing about Reading—From Book Talk to Literary Essays, Grades 3–8.* Heinemann, 2003.

Atwell, Nancie. *The Reading Zone: How to Help Kids Become Skilled, Passionate, Habitual, Critical Readers.* Scholastic, 2007.

Barlow, Carla. "Ooooh Baby, What a Brain!" *School Library Journal* (July 1997): 20–22.

Billman, Linda Webb. "Aren't These Books for Little Kids?" *Educational Leadership* (November 2002): 48–51.

Borzo, William, & Sutton Flynt. "Motivating Students to Read in the Content Classroom: Six Evidence-Based Principles." *The Reading Teacher* (October 2008): 172-174.

Bower, Bruce. "Learning to Read Evokes Hemispheric Trade-off." *Science News* (May 24, 2004): 324.

Brassell, Danny, & Timothy Rasinski. *Comprehension That Works: Taking Students Beyond Ordinary Understanding to Deep Comprehension.* Shell Education, 2008.

Carbo, Marie. *Becoming a Great Teacher of Reading: Achieving High Rapid Reading Gains with Powerful, Differentiated Strategies.* Corwin Press, 2007.

Chapman, Carolyn, & Rita King. *Differentiated Instructional Strategies for Reading in the Content Areas.* Corwin Press, 2003.

Cloues, Rachel. "Reading First, Libraries Last" (Spring 2008). Available at http://www.rethinkingschools.org.

Coiro, Julie. "Making Sense of Online Text." *Educational Leadership* (October 2005): 30–35.

Daniels, Harvey, & Steven Zemelman. "Out with the Textbooks, in with Learning." *Educational Leadership* (December 2003/January 2004): 36–40.

Dweck, Carol. "Brainology: Transforming Students' Motivation to Learn." *Independent School* (Winter 2008): 110–119.

Fisher, Douglas, Nancy Frey, & Diane Lapp. "Shared Readings: Modeling Comprehension, Vocabulary, Text Structures, and Text Features for Older Readers." *The Reading Teacher* (April 2008): 548–556.

Fogarty, Robin. *Differentiated Learning: Different Strokes for Different Folks.* Fogarty & Associates, Ltd., 2001.

Follos, Alison. "Change the Literacy Depression in Your School: Read Teens a Story!" *Library Media Connection* (April/May 2007): 20–22.

Forsten, Char, Jim Grant, & Betty Hollas. *Differentiated Instruction: Different Strategies for Different Learners, Grades K–8.* Crystal Springs Books, 2002.

Forsten, Char, Jim Grant, & Betty Hollas. *Differentiating Textbooks: Strategies to Improve Student Comprehension and Motivation.* Crystal Springs Books, 2003.

Furr, David. *Reading Clinic: A New Way to Teach Reading (Brain Research Applied to Reading).* Truman House, 2000.

Gambrell, Linda. "Reading: Does Practice Make Perfect?" *Reading Today* (June/July 2007): 16.

Gardiner, Steve. "Librarians Provide Strongest Support for Sustained Silent Reading." *Library Media Connection* (February 2007): 16–18.

Glod, Maria. "Study of Reading Program Finds a Lack of Progress." *Washington Post* (November 19, 2008): A06.

Hinchman, Kathleen, & Heather Sheridan-Thomas (eds.). *Best Practices in Adolescent Literacy Instruction.* Guilford Press, 2008.

Holland, Holly. "Reaching All Learners: You've Got to Know Them to Show Them." *Middle Ground* (April 2000): 1–3.

Hollas, Betty. *Differentiating Instruction in a Whole-Group Setting: Taking Easy First Steps into Differentiation.* Crystal Springs Books, 2005.

Hudak, Tina. "Are Librarians Reading Teachers, Too?" *Library Media Connection* (February 2008): 10–14.

Humphrey, Jack, & Leslie Preddy. "Keys to Successfully Sustaining an SSR Program." *Library Media Connection* (March 2008): 30–32.

Ivey, Gay, & Douglas Fisher. "Learning from What Doesn't Work." *Educational Leadership* (October 2005): 8–14.

Jalongo, Mary. *Young Children and Picture Books.* National Association for the Education of Young Children, 2004.

Jensen, Eric. *Teaching with the Brain in Mind.* Association for Supervision and Curriculum Development, 1998.

Johnson, Holly, & Lauren Freedman. *Content Area Literature Circles: Using Discussion for Learning across the Curriculum.* Christopher-Gordon, 2005.

Juel, Connie, & Rebecca Deffes. "Making Words Stick." *Educational Leadership* (March 2004): 30–34.

King-Friedrichs, Jeanne. "Brain-Friendly Techniques for Improving Memory." *Educational Leadership* (November 2001): 76–79.

Knowles, Elizabeth, & Martha Smith. *Boys and Literacy: Practical Strategies for Librarians, Teachers, and Parents.* Libraries Unlimited, 2005.

Knowles, Elizabeth, & Martha Smith. *Reading Rules! Motivating Teens to Read.* Libraries Unlimited, 2001.

Krashen, Stephen. "The Failure of Reading First." *Reading Today* (August/September 2008): 1.

Krashen, Stephen. "False Claims About Literacy Development." *Educational Leadership* (March 2004): 18–21.

Krashen, Stephen. "Literacy Campaigns: Access to Books is the First Step." *Literacy Network News* (Spring 2007): 7.

Krashen, Stephen. *The Power of Reading: Insights from the Research.* Libraries Unlimited, 2004.

Manzo, Kathleen. "Reading First Doesn't Help Pupils 'Get It'—Other Factors Skewing Results of Study, Federal Officials Posit." *Education Week* (May 7, 2008). Available at http://www/edweek.org/.

Manzo, Kathleen. "Studies of Popular Reading Texts Don't Make Grade." *Education Week* (August 13, 2008). Available at http://www/edweek.org.

Manzo, Kathleen. "Young People Seen Losing Love of Reading." *Education Week* (November 19, 2007). Available at http://www.edweek.org.

Miller, Donalyn. "Readers Seek Their Own Level." *Teacher Magazine* (November 4, 2008). Available at http://blogs.edweek.org/teachers/book_whisperer).

Moses, Alexandra. "Reading Round Table: Literature Circles Expand Thought." Edutopia.org (February 26, 2008). Available at http://www.edutopia.org.

Opitz, M., & T. Rasinski. *Good-Bye Round Robin.* Heinemann, 1998.

Rebora, Anthony. "Making a Difference." *Teacher Magazine* (September 10, 2008): Available at http://www.teachermagazine.org

Reis, Sally M., & Joseph S. Renzulli. *Curriculum Compacting: An Easy Start to Differentiating for High-Potential Students.* Prufrock Press, 2005.

Robb, Laura. *Differentiating Reading Instruction: How to Teach Reading to Meet the Needs of Each Student.* Scholastic, 2008.

Robb, Laura. *Teaching Reading in Social Studies, Science, and Math: Practical Ways to Weave Comprehension Strategies into Your Content Area Teaching.* Scholastic, 2003.

Routman, Regie. *Reading Essentials: The Specifics You Need to Teach Reading Well.* Heinemann, 2003.

Schweizer, Heidi, & Ben Kossow. "WebQuests: Tools for Differentiation." *Gifted Child Today* (Winter 2007): 29–35.

Sousa, David A. *How the Brain Learns to Read.* Corwin Press, 2005.

Sprenger, Marilee. *Becoming a "Wiz" at Brain-Based Teaching: How to Make Every Year Your Best Year.* Corwin Press, 2002.

Sprenger, Marilee. *Differentiation through Learning Styles and Memory.* Corwin Press, 2008.

Sprenger, Marilee. "Inside Amy's Brain." *Educational Leadership* (April 2005): 28–32.

Tate, Marcia. *Worksheets Don't Grow Dendrites: 20 Instructional Strategies That Engage the Brain.* Corwin Press, 2003.

Tomlinson, Carol Ann. *The Differentiated Classroom: Responding to the Needs of All Learners.* Association for Supervision and Curriculum Development, 1999.

Tomlinson, Carol, & Jay McTighe. *Integrating Differentiated Instruction and Understanding by Design: Connecting Content and Kids.* Association for Supervision and Curriculum Development, 2006.

Tovani, Cris. *Do I Really Have to Teach Reading? Content Comprehension, Grades 6–12.* Stenhouse Publishers, 2004.

Tyner, Beverly. *Small-Group Reading Instruction: A Differentiated Reading Model for Beginning and Struggling Readers.* International Reading Association, 2004.

Vacca, Richard T. "From Efficient Decoders to Strategic Readers." *Educational Leadership* (November 2002): 6–11.

Walpole, Sharon, & Michael McKenna. *Differentiated Reading Instruction: Strategies for the Primary Grades.* Guilford Press, 2007.

Welch, Rollie James. *The Guy-Friendly YA Library: Serving Male Teens.* Libraries Unlimited, 2007.

Wolfe, Patricia, & Pamela Nevills. *Building the Reading Brain, PreK–3.* Corwin Press & Sage, 2004.

Author Index

Index of Children's and Young Adult Book Titles

About the Author

LIZ KNOWLES, Ed.D. received her undergraduate degree in Elementary Education from Central Connecticut State University, a master's degree in Reading from Nova Southeastern University in Ft. Lauderdale, Florida, and an Ed.D. in Curriculum Development and Systemic Change, also from Nova Southeastern University. Liz has been an elementary and middle school teacher and an adjunct professor, teaching graduate courses in reading at Florida Atlantic and Nova Southeastern Universities. She served as Director of Professional Development and Curriculum at Pine Crest School, Boca Raton, Florida for 12 years. She is currently the Content Director for K-12 at Kaplan Virtual Education, a division of Kaplan University.